MANAGING *for*

OUTCOMES

Shifting from Process-Centric
to Results-Oriented Operations

WAYNE SIGLER, Ed.D.

MANAGING
for

OUTCOMES

WAYNE SIGLER, Ed.D.
University of Minnesota–Twin Cities

American Association of Collegiate
Registrars and Admissions Officers
One Dupont Circle, NW, Suite 520
Washington, DC 20036-1135

Tel: (202) 293-9161 | Fax: (202) 872-8857 | www.aacrao.org

For a complete listing of AACRAO publications, visit www.aacrao.org/publications/.

The American Association of Collegiate Registrars and Admissions Officers,
founded in 1910, is a nonprofit, voluntary, professional association of more than
10,000 higher education administrators who represent more than 2,500 institutions and agencies in the United States and in twenty-eight countries around the
world. The mission of the Association is to provide leadership in policy initiation,
interpretation, and implementation in the global educational community. This
is accomplished through the identification and promotion of standards and best
practices in enrollment management, information technology, instructional management, and student services.

LIBRARY OF CONGRESS CATALOGING-IN-PUBLICATION DATA

Sigler, Wayne, 1944–

Managing for outcomes / Wayne Sigler.

  p. cm.

ISBN 1-57858-078-1

1. Universities and colleges—Business management.
2. Operating systems (Computers)

I. Title.

LB2341.92.S56 2007
378.0068—dc22
2007026158

For my wonderfully supportive and encouraging family—my spouse, Cherryl; our son and daughter, John and Anne; brother, Lloyd; son-in-law, Wade; and grandson, Wesley.

And for my long-time mentors, teachers, and professional colleagues whose help I've been blessed with when I really needed it.

Contents

Preface

The for-profit world has always been based in the Age of Outcomes—hit the bottom line or you can't stay in business very long. That's true for owners of one-person businesses and for managers of larger enterprises.

The Age of Outcomes is now rapidly moving to the higher education, nonprofit, and government sectors. The "bottom line" for these organizations may be somewhat different than for the for-profit sector. However, in its own way, the Age of Outcomes will be as demanding and inescapable for these organizations as it always has been in the world of for-profit enterprises.

To the skeptics who believe that the work of higher education is too special or unique to measure with "bottom line" metrics, I suggest that if the cost of an organization can be assessed, it had better develop and operate with a "bottom line" focus or someone outside the organization will do it for them.

In the Age of Outcomes, organizations whose managers consistently demonstrate that they have achieved the measurable outcomes that their stakeholders value and expect will thrive. Those that cannot do so will lose both resources and influence and wither away.

This book is not intended as an indictment of higher education managers. It is instead a plea for a change in the paradigm, and ultimately the culture, of many programs in higher education from one that is primarily process-oriented to one that is more outcome-focused. I believe that many higher education managers can read the music of process yet have difficulty hearing the tune of outcomes.

Acknowledgements *iii*

I first want to thank the leadership and staff of AACRAO for making this book possible. To Jerry Sullivan, Executive Director, and Barmak Nassirian, Associate Executive Director, for encouraging me to write this book. To Martha Henebry, AACRAO's Director of Membership and Publications and AACRAO's primary leader of this project, whose professional skills and patience turned the manuscript into a book; Jacque Gourley and Paula McArdle for their editing and publication contributions.

My sincere gratitude to several people on the Admissions staff at the University of Minnesota–Twin Cities who literally helped pull this book through to completion: Jenny Mealey, for her wonderful professional skills, patience, and encouragement; Christina Boettcher for her invaluable advice and insights in helping me refine the Tri-O concept over the years; and Megan Jones for her cheerful editorial assistance. To Craig Swan, my direct supervisor at Minnesota, for his key support of the Tri-O book project.

To the following persons who graciously read and advised me on various sections of the manuscript when it was in the development stages: David Larson, Ron Matross, Jerry Rinehart, Robert Ruekert, and Dennis Skovsted.

Finally, to my fine colleagues in the Office of Admissions at the University of Minnesota–Twin Cities. I thank them for working with me on refining the various components of the Tri-O management operating system and for the outstanding contributions they make every day to the University of Minnesota and the people of Minnesota. It is a humbling and fulfilling experience to work with such fine folks.

Wayne Sigler, Ed.D
Director of Admissions
University of Minnesota–Twin Cities

About the Author

Wayne Sigler has been Director of Admissions at the University of Minnesota–Twin Cities since 1992. Prior to joining the University of Minnesota, his work in higher education included serving as Associate, then Director, of Undergraduate Admissions at the University of Maryland, College Park and Dean of Admissions/Assistant Vice President for Enrollment Services at the University of Houston. He received his master's and doctorate from The George Washington University in Washington, D.C. He is a nationally respected author, speaker, and consultant on transformational leadership, enrollment management, customer service, and recruitment.

Dr. Sigler recently served a two-year term as President of the Association of Chief Admissions Officers of Public Universities.

1

The
AGE OF OUTCOMES

Results are what count, not the number of hours or the amount of effort expended. Do not let the amount of activity distort the importance of keeping your eye on the results to be achieved.

~ EVERETT T. SUTERS (1976)

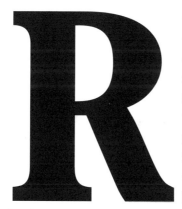

Results are absolutely essential to the viability and vitality of an organization. That may seem harsh to some of us who work in nonprofit organizations, including colleges and universities. We often believe that, unlike the business world, it is too difficult to quantify the outcomes of our work. We believe that we pass on knowledge, make new discoveries, enrich lives, heal patients, and develop future leaders: all good deeds. "How can that be measured?" we wonder.

All higher education organizations are now facing increased competition for the human, fiscal, and physical resources that are vital to keeping their programs viable. The relative scarcity of these resources,

CHAPTER 1 *The Age of Outcomes*

4

combined with a number of societal changes, is rapidly ushering in the Age of Outcomes for higher education.

In my view, the changes are so significant that the landscape of higher education will never return to the time of relatively abundant resources when a program would be adequately funded simply because it was "doing good." In the Age of Outcomes, all programs will have to demonstrate how they are "doing good" in specific, measurable terms that stakeholders value and expect.

The increased competition for scarce resources for programs such as public transportation and highways, public safety, or from the K-12 education sector and health care sectors, is making the case for higher education funding even more difficult. State leaders often believe that higher education has a significant revenue stream that it can turn to—tuition and fees—and is forcing institutions to ask their students and their families to assume a higher percentage of the cost of their education.

The percentage of state revenues that is devoted to higher education is significantly declining in many states. For example, *The New York Times* reports that "The share of all public universities' revenue deriving from state and local taxes declined to 64 percent in 2004 from 74 percent in 1991" (Dillon 2005).

A decline in state funding has serious implications for both public and private institutions. Federal and state financial aid programs, for example, have a major impact on shaping the enrollments for all segments of higher education because cost is often the overriding factor in college choice.

National Focus on Accountability

The calls for a greater focus on accountability and outcomes in higher education are numerous. The following are just three examples, among many, of major nationally-based higher education commissions addressing the issues of accountability and outcomes.

◀ The National Commission on Accountability in Higher Education (2005), a project of the State Higher Education Executive Officers (with support from the Ford Foundation), has published a report entitled, "Accountability for Better Results: A National Imperative for Higher Education." The Commission notes that:

The principles of accountability...demand action from all who share responsibility for the performance of higher education (p. 16).

The Commission also noted that several groups share this responsibility, including business and civic leaders, governors, legislators, state boards and executives for higher education, accrediting associations, the federal government, as well as higher education institutions themselves (p. 16–22).

Institutional performances goals, appropriately more detailed than state goals, must reflect the institution's mission and performance targets in instruction, research, and public service. Governing boards and administrators are responsible for creating the conditions within institutions that lead to improved performance—a focus on goals, strategic planning to improve performance, and the managerial use of incentives, rewards, and sanctions at the departmental and individuals levels.

Increasingly, institutional leadership has been measured in terms of fund-raising and other external responsibilities. These are essential functions, but better accountability for performance requires more vigorous attention to internal priorities. College and university administrators must be accountable for fostering improved performance as well as acquiring additional resources. (p. 21)

◀ The National Association of State Universities and Land-Grant Colleges has written a draft paper[1] with input from the American Association of State Colleges and Universities advocating that "Public universities and the associations that represent them should work together to develop a voluntary accountability system that would allow prospective students, their parents, and policy makers to compare similar institutions...." The draft paper "...calls for consensus on a 'meaningful but manageable' set of measures that would include student surveys, measures of student learning,

----
[1] See McPherson and Slaulenburger (2006)

and 'consumer data' on net costs, transfer and graduation rates, and postgraduate employment and earnings, among other things" (Field 2006a).

◀ The Commission on the Future of Higher Education, comprising members from the higher education and business communities, was formed by Margaret Spelling, U.S. Secretary of Education in fall 2005. Goral (2006) notes that the commission was formed to:

> *...examine an 'A list' of concerns-aid, affordability, accountability, accreditation-and develop a comprehensive national strategy for higher education that will meet the needs of a diverse population and address the economic and workforce needs of the future....*
>
> *Its recommendations...could have a long-lasting impact on higher education. And, while many within the industry believe the wake-up call is long overdue, whether those changes will be for the good of the higher education community or not is a matter of debate.*

The pre-publication Report of the Secretary of Education's Commission on the Future of Higher Education, "A Test of Leadership: Charting the Future of U.S. Higher Education," was released in September 2006. The "Recommendations" section of the Commission's Report noted that:

> *Our colleges and universities are treasured national assets, but the shortcomings we have outlined persuade us that it is time for Americans to concentrate on what higher education can become. The challenge before us is nothing less than securing the promise of the future and unleashing the potential of the American people.*
>
> *To that end, we offer recommendations that aim to improve access to higher education and make it more affordable. We seek to strengthen quality and encourage innovation. And we want to bring much-needed transparency and accountability to our colleges and universities....* (ED 2006, p. 16)

Accountability was the third recommendation of the Commission, as follows:

> *To meet the challenges of the 21st century, higher education must change from a system primarily based on reputation to one based on performance. We urge the creation of a robust culture of accountability and transparency throughout higher education.... We recommend the creation of a consumer-friendly information database on higher education with useful, reliable information on institutions, coupled with a search engine to enable students, parents, policymakers and others to weigh and rank comparative institutional performance.* (ED 2006, p. 20)

The Commission voted 18-1 to approve the report with David Ward, president of the American Council on Education, casting the sole negative vote. "Citing the report's tendency to propose 'one size fits all solutions' to problems and to minimize the financial problems facing higher education but not of the industry's own making, among other things, Ward said that he could not sign it. As the panel and Education Secretary Margaret Spellings work to further define, debate and eventually carry out the report's recommendations in the months ahead, Ward said, 'I think I can be more effective if I am free to contest some-not very many—aspects of this report.'"

The Spelling Commission Report received mixed reviews from the various associations of higher education. It is important to note that, "Hours after Ward's decision not to sign the report—a decision that he said those he polled on the American Council on Education's board had wholly endorsed—he acknowledged that it would be crucial for college officials to advocate for the commission proposals they agreed with and to work to improve the ones they don't. 'We need to find a way to show responsiveness,' he said. 'We have to create some self-generated outcomes. This is an agenda we need ownership of. If we don't, [(the commission's report] is a shot over the bow, and colleges can expect changes imposed by others.'" (Lederman 2006)

8

Marketplace Demand for Accountability

Significant increases in tuition and fees at many colleges and universities is fueling the demand of prospective students and parents for data on what returns they will realize on their investments. Specifically, they want to know about an institution's retention and graduation rates, placement rates in graduate and professional schools, and placement rates and job prospects in various career fields.

The college guidebooks have heightened the public demand for outcome data with their annual rankings of college and universities. Each publication seeks to secure its own niche in the marketplace by slicing and dicing the quantitative and qualitative information about colleges and universities.

Many people in the higher education community question the validity or applicability of rankings by college guidebooks. However, the reality is that prospective students, their parents, and higher education administrators read them. The college guidebooks, similar to consumer reports, are influential; higher education leaders who ignore their findings do so at the peril of their institution. Students and their parents have many choices and will gravitate to those institutions that best reflect their interests, needs, and concerns.

Many legislators and governors are either leading or facing a significant public resistance for increasing taxes. I am reminded of a recent meeting of the University of Minnesota Board of Regents. One of the attendees at the meeting wore a button that read, "I am a Taxpayer Watchdog." Clearly this individual was signaling his expectations for the effective use of taxpayer dollars.

Posner and Rothstein (1994) observed that the reinventing government movement popularized by former U.S. Vice President Al Gore and former government official and journalist, and now writer, David Osborne, is based on the assumption that government agencies should operate with much of the same efficiency and accountability to its stakeholders as stockholders demand from the corporate world.

Transforming inefficient bureaucracies into dynamic customer-driven organizations is challenging under any circumstances. But when the entity is something as vast and multi-faceted as the U.S. federal government, many would argue that the mechanisms for substan-

*tial change don't exist, that the problems governments must grapple
with—crime, failing schools, the health care crisis—have outstripped
its capacity to respond creatively.*

*David Osborne disagrees. Having spent the last decade studying
and writing about innovation in government and much of 1993 working as a senior advisor to the Clinton administration, Osborne is convinced that change at the federal level is not only possible but also
inevitable. In fact, he argues, many of the same tools used to improve
the performance of companies—employee empowerment, internal
competition, and measurement—can be marshaled to "reinvent" government as well.*

Aspects of this reformative movement have moved into higher
education as public officials and college and university trustees and
regents seek to apply their own corporate experience to the operation
of higher education institutions. Accrediting agencies are demanding
that institutions make outcome metrics an integral part of their governance and management processes.

Bonding agencies that rate the credit worthiness of colleges and
universities are also demanding outcome data. Even a relatively slight
improvement or decline in a college or university's bond rating can
have a significant impact on the cost of borrowing for an institution. This factor has become important enough that *The Chronicle of
Higher Education* periodically reports bonding agency decisions.

Grants by foundations and donations by private individuals have
always been extremely important to the success of colleges and universities. In an era of declining federal and state support, this source
of funding has become even more essential. At the same time, donors
are increasingly demanding data on the return, or outcome, of their
grants and gifts.

Higher Education as a Business

Business leaders often view higher education with respect for its
mission but some skepticism of its effectiveness. Charles Miller, the
chair of the National Commission on Charting the Future of U.S.
Higher Education, is a very successful businessperson who has used

the national platform of his position "…for his blunt critiques of academe and a vehicle for his big ideas."

> *From that post, he has poked, prodded, and sometimes provoked academe, challenging its "complacent," "change resistant" culture and calling for it to become more accountable to families and tax payers.*
>
> *[Miller]…scoffs at the notion that 'only the high priesthood of academia' knows how to improve higher education, arguing that colleges could learn a lot from the business world. Among his ideas: testing college students, overhauling accreditation and remaking the federal student-aid system.* (Field 2006b)

The Greentree Gazette profiled James Rogers as an example of a successful lawyer and businessman who owns 16 NBC and FOX affiliated television stations in five western states, and who serves as the chancellor of Nevada's System of Higher Education. The state system oversees two universities, four community colleges, one state college, and one environmental research institute with an overall enrollment of 105,000 students (Humes 2006).

The profile noted that Rogers is also a member of the boards of numerous universities, banks, and businesses. "He's given away and helped raise billions for various universities and has provided scholarships for students he's never met" (Humes 2006).

While clearly a strong advocate for higher education, Rogers brings a business perspective to his work as Chancellor:

> *Efficiency and productivity are big challenges for Rogers. "I don't care what you are doing, you have to put a value on your time. Academicians generally don't. Meetings that I believe could be finished in an hour last five hours. They don't understand that there is a need to be efficient even in education. They are not results-oriented. They are efforts-oriented. Academicians are more concerned with how hard they work than with what gets done. There is a big distinction there. Efforts don't satisfy the requirements of accountability. Results satisfy the requirement of accountability."* (Humes 2006)

Consultation as "Product"

The governance structure of colleges and universities usually runs on committees and task forces, and consultation is an essential component of the structure of higher education.

In the summer of 2005, the Regents of the University of Minnesota approved a major restructuring of several of its colleges and programs to help move the University to one of the top three public research universities in the world. The strategic plan was developed under the leadership of University of Minnesota President, Robert Bruininks. The plan included many significant initiatives along with the merger of three of the University's colleges with other University colleges. To secure feedback and advice on the process of implementing the decisions of the Board of Regents, the President and the Senior Vice President/Provost established 34 different task forces. In a complex institution with four campuses and over 50,000 students and 16,300 faculty and staff on the flagship campus, a large number of task forces were absolutely essential to draw out the institution's best ideas and to promote "buy-in."

The adage that people support what they help create may be time worn but remains true. Meaningful consultation is a hallmark of effective colleges and universities.

What is sometimes lost in the higher education community, however, is that consultation is only a means to an end. Consultation should lead to a plan and its implementation. Unless the outcomes of the consultative process are clearly stated and successfully implemented, nothing is accomplished. Too often, the higher education community mistakes process for an outcome.

Focusing on Activities and Process Instead of Outcomes

The corporate world clearly recognizes that it has customers. While individual businesses may not always serve their customers well, business leaders generally acknowledge that their ultimate success is tied to satisfying the expectations of their customers.

The corporate world has also long understood the importance of demonstrating a return on shareholder investments. Wall Street will pummel a company's stock price if it misses its projected quarterly earnings by even a penny. Corporate enterprises do, of course, lose their focus; however, they quickly are reminded of the penalties for doing so.

For many who work in higher education, the term "customer" seems too commercial or even demeaning. We acknowledge that we have clients, students, or patients but in our hearts we often feel they are not really "customers." At some level, we acknowledge that we must serve our clients, students, or patients but we have often not fully thought through what they really expect and value from us.

Some managers in higher education do, in fact, acknowledge the reality of having to meet the expectations of a set of obvious "customers." However, they have often not carefully identified all of the people who have a real stake in the success of their program and developed mechanisms to ensure they are consistently meeting their customers' expectations.

The outcomes of some programs in the higher education community are more easily quantified than others. Coaches are judged on their win-loss record. Development programs are assessed based on the dollars raised. Admissions offices are evaluated on the number of new students who enroll. While there are other factors that go into the assessment of these programs, the primary focus is on the bottom line.

With some exceptions, a formal, bottom-line, outcome assessment has not been used for most programs in higher education. Factors such as the centrality of a program's mission to the larger institutional mission have often been used in the budgeting process, but for the most part the assessments are largely qualitative, not quantitative.

Withering Away through Process

Many programs in higher education are either declining in influence or gradually withering away because they are not, in some cases, sufficiently focused on the achievement of specific, measurable outcomes valued and expected by key stakeholders. The gradual but clear national decline in the influence of student affairs programs over the past two decades is just one example, among many, of an undue focus on process over outcomes. (Author's note: Often colleges and universities may choose to call some programs "student affairs" and other programs "student services." Often colleges use these terms to include both groups. For purposes of this discussion, I have included both terms under the umbrella of "student affairs.")

I have a high regard for the work done by student affairs professionals. A master's degree and a doctoral supporting field in college student development have given me a strong appreciation for the importance of the work of these fine professionals to the success of a college or university. I have also spent almost my entire professional career in student affairs work. While the academic mission is, and always should be, the most important mission of a college or university, the personal and social development of students enhances the learning environment and is also clearly a significant value added to the outcomes of attending a college or university.

I recognize that there are exceptions to every generalization and I may, perhaps, oversimplify the situation. There are, of course, many effective outcome-oriented managers in the student affairs profession at many colleges and universities. For example, during my years at Minnesota, I have worked with truly outstanding chief student affairs officers and sincerely respect what they and their staff have accomplished.

For two decades I have watched with dismay while student affairs units and their constituent programs around the country have been moved further and further down in the organizational chart of many colleges and universities. Accordingly, their influence on the major decisions of the institution has also declined.

In my view, the major reason for the serious decline in influence and resources of these programs is an almost naive belief that what they are doing is so important that they have not taken the time to demonstrate, in measurable terms, how they are specifically contributing to the success of students and of the institution. Many student affairs programs refuse to acknowledge that the Age of Outcomes has arrived.

However, some student affairs leaders and educators, such as John H. Schuh (Iowa State University), M. Lee Upcraft (The Pennsylvania State University), are strong advocates of the important role that assessment should play in the student affairs profession.

14

Schuh, Upcraft, and Associates (2001), authors of *Assessment Practice in Student Affairs, An Applications Manual,* might well disagree with my fairly stark assessment of the current state of the student affairs profession. They write:

> *In general, we believe that assessment efforts can and will demonstrate the effectiveness and worth of student services and programs, and show positive relationships between students' out-of-class experiences and use of student services and programs and student learning, including academic achievement and retention...*

However, they note that:

> *Student affairs is under considerable pressure to demonstrate its importance and worth. In an era of declining resources and increased competition for what precious few resources there are, student affairs has come under the institutional financial microscope. Questions range from quality and efficiency to the ultimate question: Do we really need this service or program? So the first answer to the question, "Why assessment in student affairs?" is survival....*

Clara M. Lovett (2006), president emerita of Northern Arizona University and former president of the American Association of Higher Education, offers a very positive prescription for how student affairs professionals can better reconnect with the academic mission of their institutions and thus enjoy greater influence. Excerpts from her article, "Alternatives to the Smorgasbord: Linking Student Affairs With Learning," are included in Case Study 1 on page 18.

Activity as "Product"

Much of higher education believes that, "If we are working hard and keeping busy," an outcome is inevitable.

The sentiment behind the statement, "I could do big things if I were not so busy doing little things" is a common lament. This situation is widespread among all organizations, not just higher education. It probably speaks to the lack of getting meaningful things accomplished; working hard but not getting the really important things done!

For example, many student affairs professionals have failed to pick up the torch of leadership for crucial programs such as the retention and timely graduation of students. At many institutions, especially public colleges and universities, the retention and timely graduation of its students was not given serious attention until the college guidebooks and general media began to publicly quantify retention and graduation rates. I watched for over twenty years while the retention effort went begging for real institutional commitment and leadership at many colleges and universities.

While an effective retention program requires a campus-wide commitment and effort, student affairs professionals are well-versed in many of the key issues that impact retention. However, they have often failed to assert the necessary leadership that they could have. Today, many student affairs professionals are clearly secondary leaders in the student retention movement.

The student affairs area is just one example among many of various higher education programs that have emphasized process and activity over outcomes, to the ultimate detriment of their programs.

Even student affairs offices that have management metrics in place have often not done much better in respect to measuring specific outcomes. The managers of these programs have often focused on activity and efficiency rather than effectiveness measures. The following are several examples:

- Counting the number of students advised per day by staff members does not measure the impact of the advising sessions on the retention and timely graduation of the students.
- Cataloging the number of people who use a web-based service does not tell the story of the effectiveness of the service.
- Measuring cost savings does not address issues of effectiveness.

Even programs whose work is more easily quantified, such as those of admissions offices, often do not make significant strides in assessing the outcomes of its various admission and recruitment activities.

Doing Good while Producing Specific, Measurable Results

There are beginning to be a number of encouraging examples of programs in both higher education and other nonprofit and government agencies that are starting to demonstrate that they are not only "doing good" in line with their missions, but they are also achieving measurable outcomes. They are able to show that they are effective stewards of the resources they have been given.

Peter F. Drucker, political economist and author, is widely credited as one of the most influential pioneers in the modern study of management. In a cover story shortly after his death, *Business Week* called Drucker "The Man Who Invented Management" (Byrne 2005). *The New York Times* notes that over a 50-year career, at least half of Drucker's consulting work was done free for nonprofits and small businesses. The *Times* notes that:

> *Mr. Drucker counseled groups like the Girl Scouts to think like businesses even though their bottom line was "changed lives" rather than profits. He warned them that donors would increasingly judge them on results rather than intentions.* (Feder 2005)

A *Business Week* article on the top philanthropic donors in 2005 featured Gordon and Betty Moore. Gordon Moore is one of the cofounders of the Intel Corporation and a legend in the computer technology field. The Moores, number one in *Business Week's* 2005 list of the "50 Most Generous Philanthropists," donated almost $7.0 billion to charitable causes from 2001–2005. The authors of the *Business Week* story note that:

> *The Moores, like a growing number of big givers, take a businesslike approach to philanthropy. Rather than throwing money at problems, they try to ensure the most productive use of their dollars by funding projects they believe can produce "significant and measurable" results.* (Woolley, Hempel, and Leak 2005)

In a *Business Week* article on "Smarter Corporate Giving," Steve Rochlin, director of research and policy development at the Center for Corporate Citizenship at Boston College, sounds a similar results-oriented theme:

*Businesses succeed because they are results-oriented.... It's a waste
of resources for the community and companies not to get more rigorous
about the kind of results they want to achieve* (Byrnes 2005).

Process versus Outcomes

In this book, "process" is a shorthand and "catch-all" way of describing
an *inordinate* emphasis on procedures, rules, regulations, consultation,
and activity, and mistaking this for actual product and outcomes.

Conquering process does not mean eliminating process. Process is
not evil. In fact, process is vital and important. Process provides the
structure, order, and predictability that are absolutely essential to any
well-run organization. However, process-orientation becomes a serious
problem when its practitioners mistake the process for the outcome.

Please note that it's not that the managers with a process paradigm
don't produce results. It's that the results are often not what their primary stakeholders value or expect, or are not achieved in sufficient
amounts.

The premise of this book is that it is possible for higher education
programs and their managers to not just survive but thrive in the Age
of Outcomes! However, in order to thrive, I am absolutely convinced
that a great many higher education managers will have to make a major
paradigm shift from a process orientation to one that is stakeholder-
focused and outcome-oriented. The paradigm shift will not be easy
because for many it will ultimately require a major shift in culture.

The organizations and their managers that are able to conquer
the undue focus on process to be truly stakeholder-focused and outcome-oriented will be the ones who thrive in the Age of Outcomes.

Case Studies[2]

Many of the examples and case studies included in this book are drawn
from outside of higher education. I have done this because the examples and case studies from other fields are very helpful in providing
important perspectives on our work in higher education. For example,
the case studies drawn from the nonprofit or governmental fields are

---

[2] The case studies are quotes excerpted from various sections of articles. The quotes listed in some of the case studies
have been rearranged from their original order for purposes of clarity in preparing the case studies.

concrete examples that a paradigm change from one of primarily process to one of outcomes is possible in these types of organizations.

18

The examples and case studies in this book are used to demonstrate
that it is possible for higher education to use business techniques and
metrics to enhance effectiveness, demonstrate accountability and good
stewardship, and still stay true to the mission of the organization.

I strongly encourage you to carefully consider these examples
because they were chosen to show the relevance and contributions they
might lend to making our work in higher education more effective and
outcome-oriented. They provide excellent examples of managers that
can both read the music of process and hear the tune of outcomes.

Case
Study

CASE STUDY 1:
"ALTERNATIVES TO THE SMORGASBORD:
LINKING STUDENT AFFAIRS WITH LEARNING"

LESSONS
FOR HIGHER
EDUCATION
MANAGERS

Organizational success depends on meeting the
expectations of both on-campus and off-campus stakeholders. Organizations that don't focus
on this will lose both influence and resources.

Process and activities alone are not sufficient; they must
be combined with the achievement of outcomes that
are meaningful to the organization's stakeholders.

The following are selected excerpts from Dr. Lovett's 2006 article.
Portions that are especially relevant to this book are italicized.

Dr. Lovett observes that many American college students "...have
hovering parents who expect colleges to employ specialized professional staff to watch over their offspring. Yet most Millennials themselves prefer not to turn to those professionals to organize their
extracurricular activities and monitor their social lives...."

Attending college is an important part of the Millennials' lives, but
it is not the only thing that matters to them. As they struggle to meet
the expectations of their professors, they often must also hold jobs
because they need to earn money and have other adult responsibilities such as caring for younger siblings or their own children. Thus
they tend to ignore or resist institutional pressures to participate in
social or recreational activities that do not happen to fit their personal plans....

Lovett notes that "...the expansion of the student-affairs profession and the increased specialization within its ranks had unintended and not altogether positive consequences for the education of most American undergraduates. One result was the rise of professional silos, similar to the discipline-based academic departments that two or three decades earlier had transformed, and unintentionally Balkanized, the undergraduate curriculum. *Another unintended consequence was the separation—both psychological and organizational—between 'academics,' the purview of faculty members, and 'student life,' the purview of student-affairs professionals. Especially at large institutions, competition for student attention and institutional resources became commonplace and sometimes intense.*

Like academic departments, specialized groups within the student-affairs profession developed their own jargon, journals, conferences, and definitions of success. *If many academic departments viewed success in terms of refereed publications, student-affairs administrators measured it in terms of programs designed and activities organized. And when determining who among themselves should be promoted or otherwise rewarded, student-affairs professionals, like their faculty colleagues, found it easier to judge quantity than quality of effort. Thus, programs and activities further multiplied...."*

Lovett observes that "...most colleges today work with tight budgets....In fact, as often as not, student-affairs officers must consider trimming or even shutting down some of their programs to save money...Yet the challenge for student-affairs administrators is not simply one of cutting costs. Rather it is to refocus energies and priorities in ways that fit the views and behaviors of the Millennials, especially their refusal to conform to stereotypes about 'traditional' college students...."

"...*We must allow and encourage student-affairs professionals to refocus their energies on specific learning outcomes.* All over the country, those administrators who have advanced degrees and campus experience are more than capable of joining professors in helping students achieve their academic goals....

The time is right to tap the talents of our student-affairs experts more directly in support of teaching and learning. It is no accident that the major national organizations for student-affairs offi-cers—the American College Personnel Association and the National Association of Student Personnel Administrators—have focused both their research and their professional-development programs on student learning and assessment.... Indeed, those large and influ-ential organizations have been and remain engaged participants in higher education's major intellectual movements...."

Case Study

CASE STUDY 2:
DEMAND FOR ACCOUNTABILITY AND OUTCOMES

LESSONS FOR HIGHER EDUCATION MANAGERS	Clear examples of the need for outcomes, not just process. An example of how practitioners in a field as complex as health care are being pushed to develop meaningful outcome measures.

Regina E. Herzlinger, the Nancy R. McPherson Professor of Business Administration at Harvard Business School, has studied health care and has identified six forces that can drive health care innovation or hinder it. Most relevant to this chapter are her views on "Accountability." Herzlinger (2006) writes:

Increasingly, empowered consumers and cost-pressured payers are demanding accountability from health care innovators. For instance, they require that technology innovators show cost-effectiveness and long-term safety, in addition to fulfilling the shorter-term efficacy and safety requirements of regulatory agencies. In the United States, the numerous industry organizations that have been created to meet these demands haven't fully succeeded in doing so. For example, a study found that the accreditation of hospitals by the Joint Commission on Accreditation of Healthcare Organizations (JCAHO), an industry-dominated group, had scant correlation with mortality rates.

One reason for the limited success of these agencies is that they typically focus on process, rather than on output, looking, say, not at improvements in patient health but a whether a provider has followed a treatment process....

2

The Tri-O Management

OPERATING SYSTEM

*There's always room for improvement —
its the biggest room in the house.*

~ LOUISE HEATH LEBER

The next ten chapters of this book describe the nationally acclaimed Tri-O Management Operating System and the seven powerful components that it comprises.

Tri-O (Outcome-Oriented Operations) is an outcome-oriented Management Operating System that guides a major organizational and program paradigm transformation from a process and activity orientation to one that is focused on consistently achieving the outcomes that stakeholders value and expect.

Tri-O has been proven in actual practice to help consistently produce outstanding results. Tri-O (pronounced *Tree-oh*) is the shorthand acronym for the system.

Tri-O is a paradigm or way of looking at the world that is strongly stakeholder-focused and outcome-oriented. To be successful, an organization's managers must consistently demonstrate that they

have achieved the measurable outcomes that their stakeholders value
and expect. Those that cannot do so will lose both influence and
resources.

Tri-O is both a *working* and *aspirational* management operating
system.

A Working Management Operating System

Tri-O provides a *comprehensive* time-tested management operating system that has been applied in a "real world" setting and has been proven
to help organizations consistently produce outstanding results.

Management practitioners should think of Tri-O in terms of filling
a backpack for a journey across very challenging terrain. You want to
get from point "A" to point "B" as effectively and efficiently as possible. Filling the backpack with extraneous items, over the course of
the journey, will result in dead weight and impede progress. You want
to fill the backpack with the vital few, essential items required to successfully complete the journey.

That's what Tri-O does for higher education management. I have
distilled what it takes to be successful year after year into seven components and have further refined each component into only the vital
few absolutely essential practices that you need to be consistently
successful. I wish that I had this book when I started my higher education management career over 30 years ago.

An Aspirational Management Operating System

In my consulting work, I frequently hear both less experienced and
highly experienced managers respond to a suggestion for improvement by saying—"I know that already" or "We are already doing
that." Observations of their actual practices in many cases indicate
that they have failed to effectively implement what they may know.
Some simply seem to have stopped growing professionally.

Tri-O is also an aspirational management game plan because it is
constantly being refined as professionals grow and learn. Tri-O has
been built on trial and error and will continue to change as we find
better ways to achieve our outcomes.

The Seven Components of the
Tri-O Management Operating System

This book describes the seven components of the Tri-O Management Operating System that can help an organization and its managers realize significant and consistent success.

Each of the seven components of the Tri-O Management Operating System, its purpose and intended outcome, is described in Table 2.1, on page 26.

The seven components of the Tri-O Management Operating System are inter-related and inseparable. While your organization will definitely benefit from implementing any one of the components, the sum of the seven components, effectively applied, is greater than its individual parts.

For example, the metrics component is designed to define how success will be measured. However, unless the metrics are developed and used in concert with the other components, the metrics will be seen as numbers for numbers sake with an undue emphasis on the bottom line.

The seven components of the Tri-O Management Operating System are not an outcome by themselves. They are a means to an end—to consistently meet or exceed stakeholder expectations for measurable outcomes.

The Tri-O Outcome-Oriented Management Operating System

Tri-O is about conquering the widely held notion in higher education that process is an outcome and that everything is fine as long as the process was followed and "we worked as hard as we could and did our best."

I developed and refined the Tri-O system throughout my years of experience as a manager at five universities, and as a consultant, speaker and author. These experiences have given me numerous opportunities to observe a large number of successful, and not so successful, managers and programs and to develop a management operating system that has helped to consistently deliver outstanding results.

Tri-O will work in a program that consists of one staff member, or in very large programs. Tri-O is a way of looking at the world of work

26

in higher education and other nonprofit organizations and is not dependent on the amount of resources (human, fiscal, and physical) that are available to a particular program.

Tri-O is a proven, time tested management operating system that really works! It is a "real world" system that has helped the University of Minnesota consistently achieve outstanding enrollment success.

Recruitment and admissions at Minnesota are the result of the expertise and hard work of the entire campus, especially its colleges,

Table 2.1. *The Seven Components of the Tri-O Management Operating System*

COMPONENT	PURPOSE	OUTCOMES
Tri-O Compass	Provides clear organizational direction	◀ Gets everyone in an organization moving in the same direction to consistently achieve the outcomes its stakeholders value and expect.
Outcome-oriented Mission Statements	Describes where an organization is headed and what it plans to accomplish	◀ Identifies the organization's key stakeholders ◀ Focuses the organization and its people on achieving the outcomes valued and expected by its stakeholders
Star Tracker	Empowers an organization's people to stay on track for success	◀ Effective staff development program ◀ Effective, workable staff performance evaluation process
Outcome Planning Tools	Outlines the strategies and tactics that will be employed to achieve an organization's mission and goals.	◀ Ensuring success through effective strategic and tactical planning
Delegation	Ensures good stewardship of an organization's time and energy and the accountability for success.	◀ Reinforces that each person and each unit in an organization must contribute specific measurable outcomes that ultimately contribute to the overall success of the program. ◀ Provides a mechanism to hold people accountable for success.
Budget Stewardship	Ensures good stewardship of an organization's fiscal and physical resources.	◀ Ensures that an organization's fiscal and physical resources are effectively devoted to achieving its goals.
Metrics for Success	Defines how success will be measured	◀ Defines specific metrics so that success can be measured. ◀ Establishes accountability. ◀ Provides an early warning system to alert managers if a project is off track, thus facilitating timely corrective action.

academic leaders, and key campus services such as residential life
and financial aid, as well as the Office of Admissions.

A great deal of an institution's enrollment success can be attrib-
uted to what Kotler and Andreasen (1987) consider "...a key step in
the market planning process...developing the marketing mix...the
particular blend of controllable marketing variables that the firm
uses to achieve its objective in the target market." They also note that
the many variables that make up the marketing mix have been classified by E. Jerome McCarthy as the "four P's-product, price, place
and promotion" (McCarthy and Pennault 1987).

The competitive advantages of the flagship campus' location in the
Twin Cities, its continuing strong value despite significant tuition
and fee increases and, above all, its world class product are ultimately
the real drivers of its enrollment success. At the heart of its "product"
are its outstanding faculty, its fine students, staff, and alumni and the
special regard the people and leaders of the entire state of Minnesota
have for the place of the "U" in its culture.

A great deal of the credit for the enrollment success of the
University of Minnesota–Twin Cities also goes to the leadership of
former president, Nils Hasselmo, who pushed for major improvements in the undergraduate experience on the Twin Cities campus.
His successors, Mark Yudof and now Robert Bruininks, have continued to build on the Hasselmo initiatives while adding their own
outstanding, unique contributions. These presidents have actively
demonstrated that effective leadership really can make a difference.

To the degree that an admissions program impacts enrollment,
Tri-O has helped dramatically transform the freshman class, and the
entire campus, at the University of Minnesota–Twin Cities over the
past 14 years (1992 through 2006).

The following are some examples of how enrollment was
impacted:

◀ From 1994 to 2006, new freshman applications increased 132.3
   percent (14,045 applications).

◀ From 1992 to 2006, new freshman enrollment increased 66.6
   percent (2,175 students).

◀ Application for students of color increased 265 percent from 1994 to 2006 (+4,653 students).

◀ The enrollment of students of color increased 89 percent (+518 students).

◀ The campus achieved major increases in the academic preparedness of its new freshmen. For example, the average high school class rank of enrolled freshmen increased from 72 percent in 1992 to 83.2 percent in 2006.

The successes outlined above have been achieved at well above market-share levels. They have not merely followed rising demographics, but rather exceeded expectations.

The dramatic enhancements in the University's undergraduate student body have fueled and supported a transformation of the entire campus community. The University of Minnesota has always had an outstanding faculty and offered a world-class education, but in some ways it was primarily a commuter campus. The campus now provides an active social life for students combined with the many benefits of a major metropolitan area. The following are examples:

◀ The number of new freshmen who live on campus increased 128 percent, which has enhanced the campus community and retention rates.

◀ 59 percent of freshmen lived on campus in 1992 and now 81 percent live on campus. More than 1,700 new beds have been added on campus in the past 12 years.

◀ Retention and graduation rates have increased significantly.

◀ The enrollment success of the Twin Cities campus has attracted a substantial number of new private housing units close to campus. Approximately 3,300 new beds in housing units near campus have been added since 1996, and 1,135 housing units have been constructed in close proximity and have contributed to revitalizing businesses just off campus.

◀ The University Marching Band has increased from approximately 150 members in 1992 to a consistent membership of approximately 300 members and is again among the nation's top college bands.

◀ The Minnesota Legislature and Governor recently approved joint funding for a new University of Minnesota on-campus football stadium. Football games will move from the Metrodome to the TCF Bank Stadium in time for the 2009 football season. The open-air stadium will feature a horseshoe design and will seat 50,000 fans with the option to add 30,000 seats in the future. The Minnesota stadium will be the first new Big Ten stadium in nearly 40 years.

For the last 14 years, the University of Minnesota–Twin Cities has realized consistent outstanding enrollment success with its freshman class. A few successful years does not mean that a program is top-notch. The hallmark of an elite program is the achievement of outstanding results over a period of time through all market conditions. The Tri-O Management Operating System did not create the enrollment success, but it has been the management framework that has driven a major portion of the University's enrollment success.

Tri-O Will Work for You and Your Organization

Organizations that implement the Tri-O Management Operating System will substantially increase their chances of not only surviving, but absolutely thriving in the Age of Outcomes.

At first glance, Tri-O may appear basic. Indeed, most managers will recognize the very basic, but indispensable, elements of the 5 Ws— Who, What, Where, When, and Why—embedded into the seven components. The effective implementation of Tri-O, however, requires careful analysis, attention to detail, and the unwavering commitment of a program's leadership. For many organizations, this will require a major paradigm shift and, ultimately, a strong commitment to changing their culture.

I strongly recommend that higher education leaders, especially those who lead very successful programs, read Atul Gawande's highly compelling article "The Bell Curve, What Happens When Patients Find Out How Good Their Doctors Really Are?" (2004). While this article deals with a topic in the medical field, it has a very clear message that is applicable to all of us in higher education.

In 1964, the Cystic Fibrosis Society began to collect data on the effectiveness of treatment at all of the nation's Cystic Fibrosis (CF) centers. (This consisted of 31 centers at that time, and grew to 117 centers as of 2004.) Gawande (2004), highlighting the Cystic Fibrosis Society's findings, makes the following observations:

> *Cystic fibrosis is a genetic disease. Only a thousand American children per year are diagnosed as having it.... The gene produces a mutant protein that interferes with cells' ability to manage chloride. ...The chloride defect thickens secretions throughout the body, turning them dry and gluey.... The effects on the lungs are...what makes the disease lethal. Thickened mucus slowly fills the small airways and hardens, shrinking lung capacity. Over time, the disease leaves a child with the equivalent of just one functioning lung. Then half a lung. Then none at all.*
>
> *It used to be assumed that differences among hospitals or doctors in a particular specialty were generally insignificant. If you plotted a graph showing the results of all the centers treating cystic fibrosis—or any other disease, for that matter—people expected that the curve would look something like a shark fin, with most places clustered around the very best outcomes. But the evidence has begun to indicate otherwise. What you tend to find is a bell curve: a handful of teams with disturbingly poor outcomes for their patients, a handful of remarkably good results, and a great undistinguished middle.*
>
> *In ordinary hernia operations, the chances of recurrence are one in ten for surgeons at the unhappy end of the spectrum, one in twenty for those in the middle majority, and under one in five hundred for a handful. A Scottish study of patients with treatable colon cancer found that the ten-year survival rate ranged from a high of sixty-three per cent to a low of twenty per cent, depending on the surgeon. For heart bypass patients, even at hospitals with a good volume of experience, risk-adjusted death rates in New York vary from five per cent to under one per cent—and only a very few hospitals are down near the one-per-cent mortality rate.*
>
> *It is distressing for doctors to have to acknowledge the bell curve. It belies the promise that we make to patients who become seriously ill: that they can count on the medical system to give them their very best*

*chance at life. It also contradicts the belief nearly all of us have that
we are doing our job as well as it can be done. But evidence of the bell
curve is starting to trickle out, to doctors and patients alike, and we
are only beginning to find out what happens when it does.*

*Looking at the data over time is both fascinating and disturbing.
By 1996, mortality from CF nationally had dropped so much that
the average life expectancy had already reached ten years. (Author's
note: The author of this article pointed out that in the late 1950s, the
average patient died by the age of three.) By 1972, it was eighteen
years—a rapid and remarkable transformation.... In 2003, life expectancy with CF had risen to thirty-three years nationally, but at the
best center, it was more than forty-seven. Experts have become as leery
of life-expectancy as they are of hospital death rates, but other measures tell the same story. For example, at the median center, lung function for patients with CF—the best predicator of survival—is about
three-quarters of what it is for people without CF. At the top centers,
the average lung function of patients is indistinguishable from that of
children who do not have CF....*

*What makes the situation especially puzzling is that our system for
CF care is far more sophisticated than that for most diseases. The hun-
dred and seventeen CF centers across the country are all ultra-special-
ized, undergo a rigorous certification process, and have lots of experience
caring for people with CF. They all follow the same detailed guidelines
for CF treatment. They all participate in research trials to figure out
new and better treatments. You would think, therefore, that their results
would be much the same. Yet the differences are enormous....*

What's the point in describing an article about medical practitioners who care for Cystic Fibrosis patients in a book that primarily
deals with higher education management? The point is that *outcomes
really do matter.* In the case of Cystic Fibrosis patients, the difference
in outcomes among treatment centers can dramatically affect the
quality of life and life expectancy of its patients. Even among some
of the most highly trained and dedicated professionals in the medical
profession, outcomes can vary dramatically.

Similarly, our work as higher education managers matters a great deal to the people we serve and to our institutions. In even the most successful programs, are we absolutely certain that we have been good stewards of the finite and ever precious resources that have been dedicated to our programs? We owe it to our customers, our institutions, and ourselves to continually strive to improve our programs to ensure that we consistently achieve the outcomes valued and expected by our stakeholders.

There are highly successful programs in the higher education community that truly focus on outcomes; however, there are not enough of them. All programs, even very successful ones, must continually improve. The adage by Will Rogers, pop philosopher and comedian, is meaningful to all higher education leaders, even those at the top of their game: "Even if you are on the right track, if you just sit there you will get run over."

3

Evolution of
THE TRI-O
SYSTEM

*Life is like playing a violin solo in public
and learning the instrument as one goes on.*

35

~ SAMUEL BUTLER (1835–1902)

he Tri-O system started when I was a new and inexperienced manager searching for ways to make certain that I not only survived my various jobs, but actually thrived and did well, both for my own sake and for that of the organizations where I worked.

The Tri-O Management Operating System has been under development for many years. It is the result of my upbringing, formal education, an enormous amount of informal reading and study, and over thirty years in the trenches as a higher education manager.

Like anyone else, I was greatly influenced by my parents and my personal experiences. I worked, like so many young people of my generation, as a paperboy for three years in elementary and junior high school, delivering *The Salisbury Times.*

CHAPTER 3 *Evolution of the Tri-O System*

Reflecting back on my years as a paperboy, I recognize that *The Salisbury Times* did not impose many rules and regulations on its paperboys. My success depended simply on collecting sufficient subscription fees from my customers to pay the bi-monthly bill that was due the newspaper for the papers I was sent to deliver. This was an absolute requirement for keeping my job.

I quickly realized that my ability to pay *The Salisbury Times* the money I owed them and make any personal profit depended on recruiting and holding onto a critical mass of customers. I also learned that what the corporate world calls "bonuses" in that paper route came from the tips that some customers gave me at Christmas.

I discovered that customer service was the key to retaining customers and securing good tips at Christmas. My customers wanted their paper delivered on time, kept dry from the rain and snow, and placed on the walk or porch as each customer specified. I learned that throwing a paper on a customer's roof while riding quickly by the house on my bike was efficient but definitely not effective.

Working in my parents' furniture store in junior and senior high school, summer work in a tomato canning factory, and later driving a Pepsi truck while in college, reinforced and expanded the lessons that I had learned about customer service and expected outcomes from my paper route, specifically, the importance of retaining customers through customer service that consistently met or exceeded their expectations.

When I started working in higher education I did not think about the lessons of outcomes and customer service from my previous work experiences. I simply wanted to keep my job and earn money.

I have written this book to share with my colleagues in the nonprofit profession at-large, and specifically those who work in higher education, some of the things that I have learned in my career. I have learned a great deal from my colleagues over the years and this book is my way of returning the favor.

I want to emphasize that I have not written this book out of an arrogant sense that I have arrived as a manager and have everything figured out. I am aware of my limitations and plan to continue on my journey of striving to be as effective a manager as I can for the rest of my professional career.

Tri-O's Varied Underpinnings

For over thirty years I have looked not only to higher education but also to a variety of other fields for ideas and best practices such as the for-profit, other nonprofit and governmental sectors. For example, I have learned a great deal by reading about the world of political campaigning, the mega-church trend, the delivery of health care services and many other fields that may not, at first glance, seem to directly relate to my work but in fact offer lessons from which I have learned. I strongly believe in thinking out of the box.

Our researchers at the University of Minnesota–Twin Cities are increasingly finding the need to develop an inter-disciplinary and cross-functional approach to working on and solving various research problems. For example, our world-famous Institute of Technology has for many years included the engineering and physical sciences and mathematics under one organizational umbrella. The Institute of Technology found that having these synergistic academic departments and institutes administratively housed in one college facilitates the cross-fertilization of ideas and cooperation among the engineering and physical sciences and mathematics disciplines.

I have been influenced greatly in my thinking about management by the writings of Peter F. Drucker. Drucker's insights on management and his clarity in framing complex issues have been extremely helpful to me over my entire professional career. Many of Drucker's insights are now imbedded into my professional DNA.

I was actively involved in competitive sports for many years. Since you generally write about the things you know best, athletic examples abound in this book. Also, because athletics has prominence in our society, it is relatively easy to learn about both its successes and failures, and draw on these examples.

Business and Higher Ed: Shared Lessons

The Tri-O Management Operating System is grounded in the world of business management. It was refined in the actual practice of higher education management and reflects the importance of adapting business practices to the mission and culture of higher education to the degree they are applicable and appropriate.

Many aspects of the individual components of the Tri-O Management Operating System are not new or unique. They are drawn from many well-established management theories and practices. For example, the concepts of management-by-objectives, management-by-exception, mission statements, and strategic planning are concepts that have been outlined in management literature many times.

A Minneapolis *Star Tribune* article that featured the contrast between the work of Robert Bennett, a high-profile Minneapolis lawyer, and his everyday persona speaks to the point of doing good work while enjoying success as a business:

> *During working hours…Robert Bennett pursues gritty case after gritty case: police beatings, police shootings, the neglect of prison inmates…. Then he returns to his comfortable suburban home….*
>
> *The man behind a startling proportion of the best-known misconduct cases in Minnesota—including a $1.9 million settlement with Anoka County…is the son of a onetime executive at Target. He prefers a good steak at Morton's to an organic salad mix from Linden Hills Co-op. He has served on the board of Edina Country Club.*
>
> *There is something incongruous about his different facets. And there is something about it that makes sense.*
>
> *"Most of the 'cause' people go out of business," Bennett said. "You have to treat this as a **business**."*
>
> *The article further notes that "most of the firm's work—and most of his own—has nothing to do with civil rights or police brutality. Those cases, he said, might account for 100 percent of his headlines, but only about a third of his working hours…." (Peterson 2005).*

My interpretation of Bennett's observation is that you have to treat "doing good" as a business or you can't stay in the business of doing good. Good intentions, honorable and noble goals, and hard work are admirable, but you must be able to pay the bills.

Jim Collins, the author of the best seller, *Good to Great*, has been turning his focus to the social sector in addition to giving major attention to the world of for-profit business. While Collins (2005) acknowledges that he does not consider himself an expert on the social sectors, he views himself as a passionate student. His observations about the similarities and differences between business and the social sector are very thought provoking and, in my view, right on target. The following are selected excerpts from his monograph:

We must reject the idea—well intentioned but dead wrong—that the primary path to greatness in the social sectors is to become "more like a business." Most businesses—like anything else in life—fall somewhere between mediocre and good. Few are great. When you compare great companies with good ones, many widely practiced business norms turn out to correlate with mediocrity, not greatness. So, then, why would we want to import the practices of mediocrity into the social sector?

I shared this perspective with a gathering of business CEOs, and offended nearly everyone in the room. A hand shot up from David Weekley, one of the more thoughtful CEOs—a man who built a very successful company and now spends nearly half his time working with the social sectors. "Do you have evidence to support your point?" he demanded. "In my work with nonprofits, I find that they're in desperate need of greater discipline—disciplined planning, disciplined people, disciplined governance, disciplined allocation of resources."

*"What makes you think that's a **business** concept?" I replied. "Most businesses **also** have a desperate need for greater discipline. Mediocre companies rarely display the relentless culture of discipline—disciplined people who engage in disciplined thought and who take disciplined action—that we find in truly great companies. A culture of discipline is not a principle of business; it is a principle of greatness."*

Later, at dinner, we continued our debate, and I asked Weekley: "If you had taken a different path in life and become, say, a church leader, a university president, a nonprofit leader, a hospital CEO, or a school superintendent, would you have been any less disciplined in your approach? Would you have been less likely to practice enlightened leadership, or put less energy into getting the right people on the bus, or been less demanding of results?" Weekley considered the question for a long moment. "No, I suspect not."

That's when it dawned on me; we need a new language. The critical distinction is not between business and social, but between great and good. We need to reject the naïve imposition of the "language of busi-

*ness" on the social sectors, and instead jointly embrace a **language** of
greatness.*

40   Collins (2005) goes on to make an important observation about
the distinction between business and the social sector:

> *A great organization is one that delivers superior performance and
> makes a distinctive impact over a long period of time. For a busi-
> ness, financial returns are a perfectly legitimate measure of perfor-
> mance. For a social sector organization, however, performance must
> be assessed relative to mission, not financial returns. In the social sec-
> tors, the critical question is not "How much money do we make per
> dollar of invested capital?" but "How effectively do we deliver on our
> mission and make a distinctive impact, relative to our resources?"*

Management Consultant Frank Ostroff (2006) provides an excellent explanation of the unique mission of public-sector organizations
that I believe is applicable to higher education and the entire nonprofit sector.

> *In reality, high-performing government agencies do resemble well-
> run companies. Both have worthy goals; well-designed, rational pro-
> cesses; strict accountability; and effective leaders. But the profound
> differences in their purposes, their cultures, and the contexts within
> which they operate conjure up quite different obstacles...*
>
> *Public-sector organizations aren't created to maximize shareholder
> wealth. Rather, they are charged with promoting a particular aspect of
> the public's welfare. Effective and efficient execution of their mission is
> what taxpayers pay for....*

Higher Ed's "Customers"

While in the middle of writing this book I received a very thought
provoking e-mail from a professor at the University of Minnesota
observing that the use of the term "customer relations" in the Office
of Admissions needed to be changed to better reflect the mission
of higher education. After receiving the e-mail, I called the professor and had a very good discussion about not "Wal-Martizing" the

University and the appropriate context of customer service in the mission of a major research institution such as Minnesota.

While I use the term "customer" in this book, I intend to continue to think about the evolution of this term as it applies to higher education. Tri-O is both a working and an aspirational management operating system, and in this spirit, I will stay attuned to the need to continue to refine it.

My years in higher education have taught me to respect the difference between the mission, culture, and outcomes of higher education versus the business world. I feel strongly, however, that there are many services and programs in higher education that are, in reality, a business in a higher education setting. In these cases, it is imperative for higher education to adopt appropriate business best practices to help ensure good stewardship of resources.

For example, as a campus with over 50,000 students and 16,300 faculty and staff, the University of Minnesota–Twin Cities performs, in many ways, the functions of a sizable city. Our residence halls and apartments, food services, recreational facilities and programs, health services, and parking facilities, just to name a few, are large businesses in their own right and, for the most part, must earn their own revenue to stay in operation. It is imperative that they adopt best business practices to make certain they are serving their "customers" in an appropriate and cost-effective manner.

Case Study 3: "Using 'Business' Techniques to Wage War on Hunger" (on page 43), is an excellent example of a nonprofit applying "business techniques" to "do good" and ensure that it meets the expectation of its various stakeholders.

Viewing "Customer" as an Active Term

Terry Fiedler's (2006) article in the Minneapolis *Star Tribune* helped me crystallize my thinking about the term "customer." The article outlined how the concept of quick medical clinics is impacting the health care industry. The following are related excerpts from the article:

> *By emphasizing retail principles of price, convenience, and service,*
> *the clinics are shaking up traditional health care—from forcing doctors*

to keep longer and occasional weekend hours to helping spur more trans-
parency in pricing....

"Everybody recognizes that health care costs are out of control,"
said Minute Clinic CEO Michael Hower.... "General Motors says it
pays more for health care than steel...Starbucks pays more for health
costs than for coffee beans. I think the vision of health care as a busi-
ness proposition has the ability to change health care in the United
States...."

A study by Blue Cross and Blue Shield of Minnesota found that
the cost of a visit to Minute Clinic was about half as much as one to
a traditional clinic—$43 vs. $87. Emergency room visits for the minor
ailments can cost some $300....

Matt Kroner, Vice President of Sales for Now Medical "... argues a
dose of retail reality is just what the doctor ordered for an ailing health
care system.... Patient is a passive term.... Customer is an active
term. We never forget that the customer is paying the bill."

Kroner's focus on the active vs. passive emphasis on the person who is paying the bill—the customer—is a vital consideration here.

Higher education is a relatively unique industry because the ability to pay the bill will not, by itself, ensure admission or graduation or even a happy and positive experience. I strongly believe, however, that much of higher education is too isolated from the reality that our students and their parents are the ones who pay the bill and are, in fact, customers.

My work in admissions and enrollment management has brought home the realization that our students have choices and some freely exercise this option by transferring to other institutions. It is very disconcerting to spend a lot of time and resources to recruit a student and then have them leave the institution. Experts in commercial sales estimate that it costs as much as four to ten times as much to recruit a new customer than it does to retain one.

I intend to continue to use the term "cutomer" to encourage more higher education officials to view students and their parents in active rather than passive terms.

CHAPTER 3 *Evolution of the Tri-O System*

Tri-O: A Proven Path to Success

The rest of this book will outline the features and benefits of each of the seven components of the Tri-O Management Operating System.

By implementing Tri-O, you will:

❨ Achieve success by focusing on your stakeholders and consistently delivering the outcomes they value and expect,

❨ Better focus your organization by identifying, implementing, and tracking the vital few factors that are necessary to achieve success year after year,

❨ Save time and money because the majority of your time will be devoted to achieving results and not to managing your management system,

❨ Get everyone in your organization on the same page,

❨ Have a management operating system that was developed for higher education and is respectful of the unique mission and culture of higher education,

❨ Be in much greater control of the destiny of your organization.

This we can state with certainty: *Tri-O really works!* Our enrollment success at the University of Minnesota demonstrates this. And Tri-O can work for you and your organization.

Implementing Tri-O in your organization is well worth the effort, and you will thrive in the Age of Outcomes!

CASE STUDY 3:
USING "BUSINESS" TECHNIQUES TO
WAGE WAR ON HUNGER

LESSONS FOR HIGHER EDUCATION MANAGERS

"Business" techniques can help a nonprofit "do good" while staying true to its mission.

Nonprofits cannot simply be in the business of "doing good." They must demonstrate to their stakeholders that they are effective stewards of their resources.

A May 16, 2005 *Business Week* article featured retired Marine Corps Brigadier General, Michael P. Mulqueen, who had managed the Greater Chicago Food Depository—one of the nation's biggest hunger relief organizations—for 14 years. The following are some especially relevant excerpts from the article:

> *Nearly 14 years after the genial Mulqueen signed on, his operation has emerged as a model of efficiency for the country's food-assistance industry...*
>
> *[The]...ex-Marine runs the depository more like a business than a nonprofit. He recruited heavily from the private sector.... Mulqueen also established competitive bids on every purchase over $500 and set performance standards and rewards for his staff, to whom he pays for-profit market salaries....*
>
> *The result is a spit-and-polish operation that attracts food bank officials from around the country eager to learn how the depository does it. Among its successes: a training program in which welfare moms learn restaurant cooking while feeding hungry children through a chain of Kids Cafés; Pantry University, which teaches hundreds of volunteers to run food pantries efficiently; and the depository's new $29 million warehouse in southwest Chicago, built with the guidance of corporate logistics experts to serve some 600 local pantries and soup kitchens....*
>
> *Mulqueen and his team reflect a growing trend toward professionalization in the nonprofit world. Many groups were founded or headed by idealists ill-prepared to motivate staffs, adhere to budgets, and meet timetables. Now they increasingly embrace leaders from the outside, and résumés heavy with professional degrees and executive experience are becoming **de rigueur**....*
>
> *Mulqueen, who once commanded some 7,000 Marines and sailors in a provisioning group on Okinawa, is as demanding as any no-nonsense CEO.... His secret is combining cordiality and efficiency. Even in the military, he says, leaders don't get troops to rally around them by dictating. Leaving room for autonomy works better than simply issuing orders. And recognition matters, whether it's another stripe on a uniform or a simple "attaboy...."* (Weber 2005)

4

PURPOSE

Provides clear organizational direction

OUTCOMES

Gets everyone in an organization moving in the same direction to consistently achieve the outcomes its stakeholders value and expect

The

TRI-O COMPASS

Ideals are like stars; you will not succeed in touching them with your hands. But like the seafaring man on the desert of waters, you choose them as your guides, and following them you will reach your destiny.

~ CARL SCHURZ (1829–1906)

I t's a terrible feeling to be lost and not know where you are.

Being lost can be either physical or figurative.

As I am editing this chapter, I can see a small deer in the pasture in front of our house in the mountains of Virginia. It's a small fawn that still has its spots. It has somehow gotten separated from its mother and it is frantically running around the pasture and surrounding woods, bleating like a lamb and looking for its mother. It's raining outside and the little deer looks afraid and lost. It's a sad situation.

Hiking or camping in a large wooded area or wilderness and not knowing where you are is a physical version of being lost. At a minimum, it's highly disconcerting and fear-producing and, at its worst, it can lead to disaster.

Equally disconcerting is the way the frantic pace and details of our day-to-day work can make us lose sight of what our real work is

CHAPTER 4 *The Tri-O Compass*

all about. This is a figurative, but still very real, form of being lost. Getting so involved in the frantic pace and details of our day-to-day work so that we lose sight of what our real work is all about is a figurative, but still a very real, form of being lost. At a minimum, it's frustrating and time consuming. At its worst, it can lead to a terrible misuse of our human, fiscal, and physical resources and the eventual demise of a program and its leaders. In the Age of Outcomes, where resources are becoming increasingly scarce and expectations for outcomes are dramatically increasing, being lost can be devastating for a program and its leaders.

The centuries-old magnetic compass, and today's more sophisticated geo-positioning systems, are valuable tools for helping us to avoid getting physically lost. The Tri-O Compass is about developing a clear organizational direction.

An organization's people are the most important resources in the Tri-O management operating system. However, even great people need direction. The Tri-O Compass is designed to help get everyone in the organization moving in the same direction to consistently achieve the outcomes its stakeholders value and expect. It helps build a common organizational culture developed through a shared *philosophy* and *values* that drive the organization.

By the way, the little deer story had a happy ending. Later that day, I saw that the fawn had reconnected with its mother.

A Common Culture Developed Through A Shared Philosophy and Values

Successful organizations are based on a philosophy and values that its leaders and staff all share to a large degree. Bruch and Ghoshal (2002) state the importance of a shared vision when they quote Antoine de Saint-Exupéry:

> *If you want to build a ship, don't drum up the men to go to the forest to gather wood, saw it, and nail the planks together. Instead, teach them the desire for the sea.*

Tri-O does not require staff to agree on everything. For example, Tri-O is not about a common viewpoint on values such as religion or

[handwritten margin note: How does every decision/action contribute to student success?]

politics. The managers and staff of an organization can and should be different in many ways. They should vary in their talents and viewpoints so they can collectively use their individual strengths to offset each others' individual weaknesses. The different perspectives and creative tension that is derived from people of varying cultures and perspectives is absolutely invaluable to an organization.

While differences are healthy and productive, however, the managers and staff of an organization must be, for the most part, on the same page in respect to the philosophy and values that drive the organization. The Tri-O Compass helps get everyone to pull together for common outcomes.

In order to effectively implement the Tri-O Management Operating System, a program's leaders and staff must essentially share a common commitment to the six basic assumptions of the Tri-O system that are outlined in this chapter.

In his book, *Leadership Jazz*, Max DuPree provides a very helpful perspective on leadership with his insights on: learning from jazz band leaders, the business leader as an "orchestra conductor," and "servant leadership."

In some ways Tri-O is similar to the performance of a jazz band. The performers have different talents and roles. At times, their individual performances may seem uncoordinated. However, there is always a common theme that underpins the entire performance of a given piece of music and results in the achievement of wonderful music. With Tri-O, the underlying theme is unwavering stakeholder-focus and outcome-orientation.

Basic Assumptions of the Tri-O Management Operating System

The guiding philosophy of the Tri-O Management Operating System is based on the following six basic assumptions:

- Tri-O is stakeholder-focused and outcome-oriented.
- People are a program's most precious resource.
- Individuals must produce specific, measurable outcomes.
- There must be accountability.
- The difference between leadership and management, and the importance of both, must be understood.

◖ The difference between being efficient and being effective must be understood.

Stakeholder-Focused and Outcome-Oriented

Posner and Rothstein (1994) observe that David Osborne has focused on the process of transforming inefficient governmental bureaucracies into customer-driven organizations. Osborne looks at "…change from four thematic perspectives: customers, consequences, control and culture. First, you need to revamp the relationship between your organization and its customers…You have to ask customers what they want and then restructure your organization to deliver it."

Tri-O's stakeholder-focused, outcome-oriented paradigm is a very specific way of looking at the world of work. To be successful, an organization's managers must focus on its stakeholders and what they value and expect. A program's managers must consistently meet or exceed stakeholder expectations for measurable outcomes.

Identifying an organization's stakeholders and what they value and expect the organization to achieve is crucial to developing a stakeholder paradigm. The Tri-O approach to this process is outlined in Chapter 5, "Outcome-Oriented Mission Statements," on page 65.

People: Your Most Precious Resource

The Tri-O system celebrates the wonderful, individual talents of each team member and the importance of teamwork. The Tri-O approach to leadership and performance evaluations is outlined in Chapter 6, "Tri-O Star Tracker Component," on page 85.

Specific, Measurable Outcomes

The Tri-O paradigm requires that almost every action of an organization's staff relate to achieving the outcomes that its stakeholders value and expect. Each person in an organization must understand their role and the contributions they are expected to make to achieve the overall outcomes of the organization. Focusing on this assumption can enable an organization to *exponentially* increase its productivity and effectiveness.

Sometimes in our Tri-O workshops we use a simple exercise to emphasize this point. A penny is given to each workshop participant, skipping every third participant. We then count the total number of workshop participants and indicate that our goal is a penny from each participant.

When the workshop participants are asked to add their penny to the workshop's "treasury," it is obvious that we are short of our expected outcome. Several participants did not add their expected penny to the "treasury."

This simple exercise reflects the way any organization works. If someone does not produce his or her expected outcome, then someone else must make up for that person's shortfall. If they fail, the organization comes up short and does not meet its expected outcomes. Not meeting expected outcomes is not an option in the Age of Outcomes.

The Tri-O Management Operating System assumes that *all* staff must produce specific, measurable outcomes and Tri-O components such as outcome-oriented mission statements, metrics, and the Star Tracker approach help make this assumption a reality.

Do the practitioners of the Tri-O system reach the goal of having each staff member achieve high levels of measurable productivity? Unfortunately, no! But Tri-O can help an organization make major strides in productivity and effectiveness.

Accountability

I have learned that if everyone is accountable, no one is truly accountable. Implementing a clear culture of accountability is imperative in the Tri-O system.

Committees and task forces definitely have their place in higher education management. However, a possible downside of collective responsibility is often a lack of accountability for real outcomes.

An example from the corporate sector reinforces the importance of accountability. Hewlett-Packard (HP), the computer and printer corporation, ran into problems with its performance and profitability. HP turned to a new CEO, Mark V. Hurd, to turn the situation around.

The new CEO's "…most sweeping initiative is to rebuild the culture of accountability that once made HP one of tech's most consistent performers." Hurd tossed out the matrix management structure favored by the former CEO "...which muddied responsibilities, to give business heads more control of their units. 'The more accountable I can make you, the easier it is for you to show you're a great performer' says Hurd. 'The more I use a matrix, the easier I make it to blame someone else.'" (Burrows 2005, p. 83)

Booz Allen Hamilton consultants Gary L. Neilson and Bruce A. Pasternack have identified ten traits that most organizations they characterize as "resilient" generally exhibit. In describing Neilson and Pasternak's work, Paul Michelman (2005), the editor of the *Harvard Management Update*, noted that, "Depending on who is doing the describing, a 'resilient' organization is one that is steadfast enough to weather turbulent times yet flexible enough to change when change is necessary. Indeed, by some definitions, resilient organizations are characterized by their ability to change before change becomes crucial."

In their book, *Results: Keep What's Good, Fix What's Wrong, and Unlock Great Performance*, Neilson and Pasternak (2005) note that one of the ten important traits of a resilient organization is the building of a culture of commitment and accountability:

> *All organizations make commitments. It's how they define these commitments, translate them into decision rights, and measure performance against them that distinguishes resilient organizations. Commitments and the decision rights that result are not soft or subject to interpretation; they are etched in stone and obvious to all, particularly to the individuals held accountable. In fact, a resilient organization's commitments are hard currency backed by the "gold standard" of full and clear accountability.*

Implementing a culture of accountability will require a significant paradigm shift for many higher education programs. Embracing this concept can be somewhat controversial because it will often challenge long-held viewpoints about a staff member's real work and their responsibility to produce specific, measurable outcomes.

"Case Study 4: Asking Very Difficult Questions," on page 57, outlines how a St. Paul, Minnesota Police commander asks the following question of the members of his Parking Enforcement Unit: "If you're working a full shift and only have six violations, what are you doing with the rest of your time?" (Padilla 2006)

I believe that all of us in higher education must ask ourselves and our colleagues this very sensitive question. In some ways this question is like the elephant in the room that everyone is trying to ignore. However, in the Age of Outcomes, all higher education managers must ask this question in a respectful but direct manner.

The Tri-O Star Tracker component, outlined in Chapter 6 (on page 85), is based on helping people be successful and not concentrating on finding fault. However, once the program's managers have given a project leader or staff member sufficient resources and support, the person must be held accountable for achieving the expected outcomes. The alternative is either failure or mediocre results, which is simply not acceptable in the Age of Outcomes.

Tri-O encourages and celebrates teamwork. Teamwork, combined with individual accountability, is a major key to an outcome-oriented approach to leadership. However, one person must ultimately be accountable for each activity, project, and unit in a Tri-O organization.

Leadership versus Management

Harvard University business professor and author, John P. Kotter, is acknowledged as one of the premier authorities on the practice of leadership and management. Kotter (1990) asserts:

> *Management is about coping with complexity.... Without good management, complex enterprises tend to become chaotic in ways that threaten their very existence. Good management brings a degree of order and consistency to key dimensions like the quality and profitability of products.*
>
> *Leadership, by contrast, is about coping with change.... More change always demands more leadership.*

As Kotter (1990) points out:

> *Leadership is different from Management, but not for the reasons most people think. Leadership isn't mystical and mysterious. It has nothing to do with having "charisma" or other exotic personality*

traits. It is not the province of a chosen few. Nor is leadership neces-sarily better than management or a replacement for it.

Rather, leadership and management are two distinctive and com-plementary systems of action. Each has its own function and char-acteristic activities. Both are necessary for success in an increasingly complex and volatile business environment.... The real challenge is to combine strong leadership and strong management and use each to balance each other.

Placing Kotter's definitions into the context of higher education, I believe that leadership is about providing the vision and focus to deter-mine where the institution is headed, who it is serving, what outcomes the institution's stakeholders value and expect, and how it can stay relevant as conditions change. Effective management is about mak-ing certain the institution effectively employs its resources and consis-tently achieves the outcomes that its stakeholders value and expect.

An effective organization must recognize the difference between leadership and management and make certain that its staff collec-tively implement both sets of skills. Tri-O is termed a *management operating system*, but in this case, "management" is a catch-all short-hand for a comprehensive operating system that will not work unless both essential skills are consistently implemented.

Additional thoughts on leadership and management are found throughout this book, especially in Chapter 6, "Tri-O Star Tracker Component," on page 85.

Efficiency versus Effectiveness

Peter F. Drucker (2006) says "efficiency is doing things right; effec-tiveness is doing the right things."

In his writings, Drucker frequently addresses the implications of being effective vs. being efficient. And in the Office of Admissions at the University of Minnesota, we also spend a lot of time talking about the difference between being "efficient" and being "effective." It is, of course, very important to be efficient because people's time and energy and fiscal and physical resources are precious in any organiza-tion. However, if we chase efficiency without regard to what we must really accomplish for our stakeholders, it is false economy.

It is very easy for organizations to mistake process for outcomes by not understanding that efficiency does not always equate to effectiveness. While an organization should always strive for efficiency in its work, it is more important to insist on effectiveness. Being effective requires the manager to build in efficiency to the highest degree possible. Efficiency should definitely not be ignored or neglected. However, achieving outcomes that our stakeholders value and expect is more important than simple efficiency.

There is a saying in golf that you "drive for show and putt for dough." Essentially, this means driving the golf ball a long distance is very dramatic and can evoke great admiration from fans and fellow golfers. Putting is much less dramatic except for the rare, exceptionally long, putt that drops in. However, experienced golfers know that the real opportunity to score well in golf comes not from long drives but the less dramatic but more effective result of staying in the fairway and putting well. Sure, a long drive is an advantage, but what's really most important is to keep the ball straight, in the fairway, and out of trouble. Consistent putting, while not as dramatic as a long drive, adds up to winning golf.

The golfers' saying is also relevant to management. In my view, concentrating on efficiency is like concentrating on long showy drives in golf. On the surface, dramatically cutting costs and process time makes a compelling short-term story. But in the long run, it is being effective that leads to consistent success. Usually, an undue emphasis on efficiency benefits the organization but not the stakeholder.

Since I have been at the University of Minnesota, I have received my health care through a large health maintenance organization (HMO). The HMO is one of the options offered by the University health plan.

For the first several years, I really disliked working with the HMO. Prior to joining the HMO, I had worked primarily with doctors of my choice—generally ones that I could relate to. I felt that the HMO was disinterested and much more focused on efficiency than on me as an individual. I respected the quality of the clinical care but I really felt like a number instead of an individual.

This all changed when I found a dentist at the HMO that I really liked. He combined outstanding clinical care with personal warmth and genuine interest for my concerns. I then found an internal medicine doctor at the HMO that approached his work in the same fashion as my dentist. The staff that work with my dentist and doctor use the same approach in their work.

Once I began to develop a relationship with the HMO through my dentist and doctor, I could then see some significant advantages to belonging to the HMO. Now I view the HMO as my friend. Because my dentist and doctor care about being effective in relationships and not just clinically competent and efficient, my whole view of the organization changed from that of a very reluctant customer to a strong advocate.

I strongly believe that striking an appropriate balance between efficiency vs. effectiveness is a major problem for institutions of higher education. When higher education organizations develop outcomes assessment measures, they often concentrate and focus on efficiency and activity measures rather than effectiveness measures.

Activity and efficiency measures often include the number of students served by the program, budget allocation by function, and staffing levels. Efficiency measures usually describe process and activities. While these measures provide useful information, they do not indicate the degree to which a program has been a good steward of the fiscal, human, and physical resources allocated to it.

The Tri-O system is based on being as efficient as possible but with priority given to being effective so that expected outcomes are achieved.

Case study numbers 5, 6 and 7 offer real world examples of the importance of striking an appropriate balance between efficiency and effectiveness.

Getting Everyone Moving in the Same Direction

The Tri-O Compass helps get everyone in an organization moving in the same direction to consistently achieve outcomes that its stakeholders value and expect.

The guiding philosophy and values of the Tri-O Management Operating System are based on the six basic assumptions that have been described in this chapter. Effectively leading your staff through the steps of operationalizing the six basic assumptions of Tri-O will result in the very real outcome of strengthening your program's culture through a shared philosophy and values.

Just as the older magnetic compass or the more modern geo-positioning systems are very basic tools in finding your way through confusing physical territory, the Tri-O Compass will help your organization stay on course in the highly demanding Age of Outcomes.

CASE STUDY 4:
ASKING VERY DIFFICULT QUESTIONS

LESSONS
FOR HIGHER
EDUCATION
MANAGERS

Reinforce the importance that each member of an organization produces measurable outcomes.

Changing a paradigm and culture often requires a willingness to ask difficult questions.

"If you're working a full shift and only have six violations, what are you doing with the rest of your time?" (Padilla 2006)

The question raised by St. Paul Minnesota Police Commander Eric Anderson in response to questions and criticism about his setting "…a job performance standard that each officer write up, on average, 55 violations per shift" is one that is often very difficult for managers in the higher education, governmental, and nonprofit sectors to ask. However, it's one of the essential questions that the corporate sector has often asked and it's now part of the larger questions that stakeholders (such as taxpayers) are clearly expecting the nonprofit sector to answer—How can we demonstrate that we are using our resources effectively?

Padilla (2006) points out both the pros and cons of asking such a question, noting that—

> *The idea that St. Paul parking enforcement officers are stealthily hunting for violators to pounce on is shared by many who find the envelopes on their windshields. [Cmdr.] Anderson laughs at assertions that his 55-violations-per-day mandate will lead to officers waiting at a meter, [watching] for it expire. "It was meant as a way to measure performance," he said. Anderson followed up his comment with the question listed at the top of this case study.*

The article also features Officer George Castillo, the top performer in 2005 based on the most citations in the unit.

> *He'll listen to expired meter stories. People who say they went for change and can pull out a fistful of coins to prove it have a shot at getting off with just a warning.*
>
> *But arguing with clichéd excuses about how the meter must have expired just a minute ago? Those violators get advice on how to dispute the fine.*
>
> *As he walked the beat Thursday, Castillo gave a good share of warnings, moving drivers along from areas where parking or stopping is restricted.*
>
> *Does he ever have to sit and wait for meters to expire?*
>
> *"I don't have to," he said. "There's going to be an expired meter on the next block."*
>
> *As Castillo patrolled on the Thursday covered by the reporter, "He gave little thought to the 55-violation quota. In 90 minutes, he wrote 17 tickets for 18 violations, well on pace to achieve the goal."*

Case
Study

....
CASE STUDY 5:
"ONE STOP" CENTERS—EFFICIENT OR EFFECTIVE?

LESSONS
FOR HIGHER
EDUCATION
MANAGERS

Focusing on effectiveness and not primarily efficiency is imperative for the success of an organization.

It is much easier for an organization to choose short-term efficiency rather than effectiveness, but in the longer term it extracts a much higher price.

Nationally, there is a current trend toward moving key student services such as registration, records, financial aid, and the bursar function into a "one-stop" center. The "one-stop" concept is often implemented as a physical location or as a web-based approach or a combination of the two. The most effective "one-stop" centers combine both approaches.

The one-stop approach holds enormous opportunities for enhancing efficiency; I am a proponent of this concept. At the same time, I believe the one-stop concept can face significant challenges to increasing effectiveness.

It is very easy to rack up impressive cost savings when efficiency replaces effectiveness by "driving" customers to the web or having inordinate wait times on the call center phone lines. Effectiveness in a one-stop center depends on what its customers want to accomplish at the time. Customers usually do not mind dealing with a one-stop center for relatively straightforward transactions such as address changes or changing courses. Many customers also do not mind, and may prefer, applying for admission, financial aid, scholarships, honors and campus housing, or registering for classes, via the web.

The preference of some customers for using technology to obtain services was reinforced by Dan McElroy, senior advisor on innovation to Minnesota Governor Tim Pawlenty:

> ...[W]e're finding increasingly that talking to a human being is not people's first choice. For more and more people, they want to receive the service as quickly and efficiently as possible, and they're accustomed to doing it online, and if that's the simplest, that's their preference. (Hage 2006)

The real issue seems to be distinguishing between handling a transaction versus dealing with a more complex issue or building a relationship with an institution. Dealing with a different representative each time a customer contacts the one-stop center by phone or e-mail can be frustrating if the issue is relatively complex or sensitive and cannot be resolved via the web.

Effective enrollment managers clearly understand that they must develop a relationship with prospective students in the recruitment process if they hope to enroll the prospect. They can direct the prospect to the web for basic transactions; however the goal in recruiting is to have each transaction or recruitment contact move the prospect to the next level of commitment to the institution. Effective enrollment managers care deeply about providing appropriate options for customer service not only because it is the right thing to do but also because they are measured on the outcomes of their programs.

In a *New York Times* article entitled "Your Call Should Be Important to Us, but It's Not," Taylor (2006) addressed the frustrations that consumers often have with poor customer service, such as breaking through automated interactive voice-response systems to speak with a human being. The article cited the findings of Richard Shapiro, president of the Center for Client Retention in Springfield, New Jersey:

> *You create more value through a dialogue with a live agent.... A call is an opportunity to build a relationship, to encourage customers to stay with the brand. There can be a real return on this investment.*

Taylor (2006) commented on Mr. Shapiro's viewpoint on the importance of customer contact with a human representative of a company:

> *It's a point that too many cost-conscious companies seem willing to overlook. In an era of fierce competition, when customers have more choices than ever, the toughest business challenge isn't to keep expenses down. It's to keep loyalty high. Anything that a company does to make its products and services a little more engaging, a little less ordinary, can pay big dividends. Anything like, say, answering the phone.*

It is my opinion that institutions that have relatively low rates of retention and timely graduation exacerbate the problem by unduly relying on one-stop centers for efficiency when many situations demand an appropriate balance between "high touch" and "high tech" approaches. I would be surprised if the vast majority of one-stop centers are regularly evaluated on effectiveness measures. This is not to suggest that managers of one-stop centers do not care about effectiveness and about good customer service. Rather, it's more likely a case of the paradigm used to build and evaluate the one-stop center—efficiency or effectiveness.

CASE STUDY 6:
A WORLD-RESPECTED AND HIGHLY
SUCCESSFUL CORPORATION REEVALUATES
ITS EFFICIENCY-RELATED EFFORTS

Case
Study

LESSONS
FOR HIGHER
EDUCATION
MANAGERS

Efficiency by itself is not sufficient; effectiveness
is necessary to produce expected outcomes.

Stakeholders matter!

In its March 6, 2006 issue, *Fortune Magazine* named the General
Electric Company the most admired company in America for the
sixth time in the past decade. The article notes that "GE has also
ranked No. 1 in the *Financial Times'* 'most respected' survey for seven
of the past eight years, and it topped a recent Barron's ranking of
most admired companies" (Colvin 2006).

The *Fortune* article heaps more praise on GE:

> *But why does the world love this company so much?.... The answer
> lies in the fact that our survey (like the others) is a poll not of consum-
> ers but of businesspeople working in the same hard world as GE....
> Through good years and bad, GE consistently does things the rest only
> wish they could.*
>
> *For the past century or so, for example, GE has continually set the
> agenda of management ideas and practices that other companies will
> follow. Practically everyone in business realizes this. GE's record of
> being ahead of the game is remarkable.* (Colvin 2006)

I include the very positive article about GE in this case study
because in the business world people watch and follow GE's practices
closely. Therefore, when Arussy's 2005 article in *Customer Relationship
Management* pointed out that GE is reevaluating its vaunted efficiency-
related efforts, it caught my attention. Here are a few excerpts from
the very compelling article:

> *General Electric CEO Jeffrey Immelt is willing to face what most
> CEOs are still hiding from: Efficiency has come at the expense of the
> customer.... The company once known for absolute efficiency (Six
> Sigma-based processes) has finally discovered that having a good*

62

product is simply not enough these days. Tightly designed, efficient processes and methods alone just don't seem to catch a customer's eye.

The search is not exclusive to GE. Growth-and-innovation is today's mantra; the pendulum has swung from cost reduction back to growth in the past few years....

*[G.E. CEO] Immelt has recognized that efficiency is appealing, but not the goal; and that efficiency-related efforts will most likely **damage** customer values and customer willingness to do business.*

**Case
Study**

CASE STUDY 7:
HOW COST-CUTTING
CAN BACKFIRE WHEN IT IGNITES CONSUMER RAGE

LESSONS FOR HIGHER EDUCATION MANAGERS	Stakeholders matter!
	An organization must respect and care for its people.
	Effectiveness must not be neglected by unduly chasing efficiency.

Hindo (2006) provides a dramatic contrast of what happens when companies get it right with the customer experience and when they don't:

The feeling of frustration provoked by rude service, long lines, ignored complaints, unanswered questions, and interminable phone delays is supposed to be a thing of the past. This is a golden age for consumers, right? It's the era that has spawned a 24/7 convenience economy dedicated to satisfying the time-pressed, hyper-informed, ever-demanding American public. But some companies haven't received that memo...Home Depot, Dell, and Northwest Airlines.

They operate in disparate industries, but each has fallen victim to a seductive fiction; that customer service and operational efficiency are mutually exclusive....

The upshot is that some companies, in their passion to drive down costs, have mangled their relationships with customers. The three melt-downs described here are all cases in which executives have lost track of the delicate balance between efficiency and service. "In the short term, most companies would say it is appropriate" to trade services for penny-pinching, says Valarie Zeithaml, a marketing professor at the

*University of North Carolina. "That is always a shortsighted view. It
inevitably harms customer satisfaction in the long term."*

*Smart companies-Southwest Airlines Co., and Costco Wholesale
Corp., to name two standouts-have it both ways. Well-trained workers equal fewer complaints. That means lower costs, a workforce free to
make more sales, and happier customers willing to spend more money
and tell their friends about it later....*

*Each of the three companies is responding to its problems differently.
Home Depot seems finally to realize that it needs to make a change;
Dell, whose market share has already slipped, is trying to put the genie
back into the bottle; and Northwest is in such a desperate fight for survival that it doesn't seem to care. While this trio struggles, savvy com-
petitors are doing all the little things that make their stuff more fun
to buy. Customer "experience matters," says Andy Fromm, president
of the Service Management Group. "Most companies get it." Clearly
some still don't.*

5

PURPOSE

Describes where
an organization is
headed and what it
plans to accomplish

OUTCOMES

Identifies the
organization's key
stakeholders

Focuses the organization
and its people on
achieving the outcomes
valued and expected
by its stakeholders

Outcome-Oriented

MISSION STATEMENTS

*I don't know the key to success, but the
key to failure is to try to please everyone.*

~ BILL COSBY (2007)

"An employee of a national mobile communication corporation whose boss told him to memorize the corporation's credo says, 'They give you this statement, laminated to a little card. You're supposed to keep it on you at all times, in case somebody from corporate comes by and asks you to recite it.

"'It is, in my view, a crock of sh★★. Not so much because of what's on the card. It's that the company is forcing this on you—they're throwing up all over you with their philosophy. I'm good at my job. I've been promoted three times. All I want is to go out and do it, without some idiot in a leather chair telling me how to think'" (Farnham 1993).

When most faculty and staff in the higher education community hear the term "mission statement" their thoughts may not be as emotional and stark as the employee quoted above. However for most

CHAPTER 5 *Outcome-oriented Mission Statements*

68

people, their experience with the process of developing a mission statement often resulted in:

◀ Frustration with the time spent on a seemingly pointless exercise;

◀ Frustration with the difficulty of trying to get everyone on the same page;

◀ A document that is so long and complicated that almost no one can remember what it said; and finally,

◀ The mission statement being filed and promptly forgotten.

The Mission Statement's Purpose

A mission statement is about what the organization wants to achieve. Jeffrey Abrahams (1999), author of *The Missions Statement Book: 301 Corporate Mission Statements from America's Top Companies*, observes that:

> *[A] Mission statement can inspire employees across an organization and remind them of the purpose of the company and each individual's role in achieving the goal.*

Peter F. Drucker (1990), the person referred to by *Business Week* as "The Man Who Invented Management…," is clear about the importance of a mission statement:

> *Performance in the non-profit institution must be planned. And this starts out with the mission. Non-profits fail to perform unless they start out with their mission. For the mission defines what results are in this particular non-profit institution. And then one asks: Who are our constituencies, and what are the results for each of them?*

My experience of working and consulting in the higher education community for many years has led me to concur with these authors regarding the importance of an effective mission statement. It's vital that everyone in an organization know where their organization is headed and what it plans to achieve. To do this, it is imperative that each unit within the larger organization have an *effective* mission statement. The manager of each unit must also have his or her own mission statement and, ideally, each staff member should have his or her own mission statement.

I am reasonably certain that most faculty and staff in a college and university cannot easily summarize the mission statement for their institution. I also am fairly certain that most colleges and departments within an institution do not have a useable mission statement. This is one of the reasons why colleges and universities are often so process- and activity-oriented rather than outcome-oriented.

I believe that most faculty members are very outcome-oriented in a great portion of their work because, to some degree, they are relatively independent contractors working within an academic department. They generally seek out exactly what it takes to gain tenure or to secure promotion to full professor. Despite often being mixed with institutional politics and personalities, the tenure, promotion, and grant and research funding processes are quite Darwinian, especially in the very best institutions.

I have a tremendous respect for the faculty in American higher education and believe that their focus on their individual achievement, combined with outstanding training and talents and commitment to improving society, makes them the best in the world in contributing to their institutions and society in general. The faculty represents the core "product" that an institution offers to its students.

It is when the individual faculty member moves into his or her role as a member of their department or the larger institution that the mission and focus on real outcomes sometimes begins to break down because of the lack of a coherent unifying mission at the department, college, or institutional level and, at times, lack of effective leadership.

I am far less sanguine about the clarity of mission and focus on outcomes in the administrative units of most colleges and universities. I believe that America's colleges and universities are blessed with highly talented and committed staff who generally do a great job for both their institution and society in general. I believe that many staff members, in their own sphere of work, are as talented and committed as the very best faculty members. What they often lack is the clarity of mission and personal accountability that individual faculty have in respect to their own personal advancement. This is where effective leadership and the direction provided by effective mission statements are so crucial.

70

Effective Mission Statements

An effective mission statement is not a luxury but an absolute necessity if the organization hopes to conquer process and manage for the outcomes that its stakeholders value and expect.

Although developing effective mission statements takes time, skipping the step of developing an effective mission statement is like designing a road map without knowing the destination. A mission statement translates the organization's vision into concrete terms it can understand and follow.

I have found the process of developing an organizational mission statement and talking with our staff about their mission statements to be almost as valuable as the product of a mission statement itself. (Please note: I recognize that process has an important place in the work of an organization!) Job descriptions are generally only useful when a person begins a job. Over time, the requirements of the job change and the infamous "other duties as assigned" expand. Taking the time to think about your duties and what you really have to accomplish to be successful is invaluable.

The Star Tracker Component, described in Chapter 6 (on page 85), is built on the premise that most of us want to do a great job. Sometimes when our outcomes are not on target with our stakeholders' expectations it's because we really haven't spelled out in writing exactly what our job is and the outcomes for which we are responsible. Also, we can be overwhelmed with the pace and demands of our job and lose our focus.

Following the guidelines that are outlined in this chapter will ensure that you and your organization will know where it is headed in order to use the essential outcome-oriented mission statement to achieve its major outcomes.

The "Strategic Service Vision"

I urge you to read the work of James L. Heskett, Professor Emeritus at the Harvard Business School, because it is extremely helpful in making the case for organizations (both for-profit and nonprofit) to develop results-oriented missions if they want to be truly successful.

Heskett developed what he terms the "strategic service vision": "...a set of ideas and actions that maximizes the leverage of results over efforts directed toward well-defined targets and supported with highly focused operating strategies." Heskett writes that the framework, "...evolved from my efforts to document factors in the success of outstanding entrepreneurial endeavors, those that have literally changed the standards for performance in their chosen fields."

Heskett outlines four examples of outstanding social entrepreneurs who have a strategic service vision:

◀ Dr. Byrnes Shouldice, founder of Shouldice Hospital.
◀ Commissioner William Bratton, head of the New York City Police department from 1994-1996.
◀ Frances Hesselbein, executive director of the Girl Scouts of the USA between 1976 and 1991.
◀ Bill Strickland, Jr., founder of the Manchester Craftsman Guild in Pittsburgh, Pennsylvania.

Heskett (2002) also outlines what he terms a "gem of wisdom," which reinforces the importance that organizations must produce outcomes:

An old marketing saw tells us that, "Customers don't buy quarter-inch drills, they buy quarter-inch holes." The lesson here for profit-making organizations is that if you think that you are in the business of delivering quarter-inch drills, you run the risk of being put out of business by someone who devises a method for making holes more effectively and efficiently. The lesson is just as important for enterprising nonprofit entrepreneurs.

Failure to define the mission of the organization in terms of results for each of its important constituencies can produce a strategy irrelevant to the needs of clients, the most important constituency of all... in one way or another, those associated with every leading service organization my associates and I have studied over the past 20 years understand it. The challenge for all us is to act on this understanding.

Characteristics of an Effective
Outcome-Oriented Mission Statement

Developing effective mission statements is an integral part of the Tri-O Management Operating System. It must be acknowledged, however, that this seemingly simple process can be one of the most difficult steps in implementing the Tri-O system because it takes time and effort to develop a mission statement that will really be useful in guiding the organization and its sub-units.

An *"effective"* mission statement must be:

◀ Specific—Identify the specific outcomes the unit will achieve.

◀ Applicable—Usable in everyday operations.

◀ Memorable—Stated in five to 15 words.

Specific

Drucker (1990) points out that, "The task of the non-profit manager is to try to convert the organization's mission statement into specifics."

It may take a considerable amount of time to sort out the actual outcomes the organization should achieve rather than focusing primarily on the organization's processes and activities. However, higher education managers must spend the time necessary to identify the specific outcomes that the organization will achieve or they will not maximize the use of the resources that have been assigned to them.

The Tri-O system is stakeholder-focused, and outcome-oriented. Therefore, the process of developing a mission statement begins with identifying the organization's stakeholders and what each group expects the organization to achieve—the organization's outcomes. This planning exercise must ultimately lead to the identification of specific outcomes that can be measured.

Applicable

A mission statement that cannot be used is worthless.

> *A mission statement has to be operational, otherwise it's just good intentions. A mission statement has to focus on what the institution really tries to do and then do it so that everybody in the organization can say, "This is my contribution to the goal."* (Drucker 1990)

Much of the work of an operational manager in any organization is binary. A manager must decide "yes" or "no" to numerous questions and issues every day in respect to the actions that will or will not be taken. To be effective in a binary environment, the mission statement must relate to the everyday work of the organization and guide its hour-by-hour, day-to-day work.

It is imperative that the persons involved in developing the mission statement be able to see that it will help make their work more meaningful and productive.

Memorable

Unless the mission statement is brief enough to be remembered by everyone in the organization, it will be useless. Trial and error has led me to conclude that five to 15 words is the optimal length of an effective mission statement.

Even conscientious staff members will not search out a mission statement they cannot remember. Unless the staff can remember the mission statement, they will not use it.

The fewer words the better!

Sample Mission Statements[3]

Office of Admissions

For over a decade, the mission statement of the University of Minnesota–Twin Cities Office of Admissions has been:

◀ The Office of Admissions will take leadership in bringing to the University the number and types of students who will benefit both themselves and the University by their enrollment.

◀ To do this, we will consistently provide "extra-mile customer service."

Distilled to fit the five to 15 word test, the mission statement reads: "Consistently hit the numbers through providing 'extra-mile' customer service."

---

[3] Source: University of Minnesota–Twin Cities Office of Admissions. It is important to note that the mission statements listed as examples do not address the important questions of how the goals will be achieved but rather what the office's, unit's or project's specific expected outcomes are.

Director of Admissions

I developed the following mission statement to guide my work as Director of Admissions:

74

- ◀ Lead
- ◀ Hit the numbers
- ◀ Keep people out of the President's Office
- ◀ Maintain stakeholder confidence

My experience in enrollment management has led me to the absolute conviction that no matter what other directives I get from the institution's leadership, the four items listed in my mission statement are absolutely imperative for the office to be viewed as consistently successful. They are the four keys to surviving in my position.

My personal mission statement for my role as Director of Admissions reflects my responsibility to:

- ◀ *Provide leadership for the Office of Admissions.* While the director of an admissions office clearly has managerial duties, the role of director is primarily about leadership. This entails duties such as establishing a vision, setting direction and strategy, and obtaining and focusing resources. I must make certain that our office achieves its goals for the current year and, at the same time, concentrate on the actions the office must take to achieve its expected outcomes in each of the next two years.

- ◀ *Consistently hit the enrollment goals.* A director of admissions does not keep his or her position very long unless the numbers are consistently met. Period.

- ◀ *Keep people out of the President's Office.* Having the President and/or his or her staff constantly hear complaints about an office is a certain way to erode their confidence in the office. While a few complaints are probably inevitable, frequent complaints are corrosive. The director and staff must do its work in a customer-focused and honorable manner so that its external customers (*e.g.,* prospective students and their parents) and its on-campus customers (*e.g.,* deans) feel that they are being heard and well served. While the applicant and the parents may not agree with an unfavorable decision on the application for admission, the admissions staff must work with them so that they understand they were treated fairly, consistently, individually, and respectfully.

◀ *Maintain stakeholder confidence.* It is imperative that the Office of Admissions know what its stakeholders value and expect from the office, to consistently deliver on those expectations, and keep the stakeholders updated, informed, and confident that expectations are being achieved.

Admissions Staff

A sample of some of the other individual mission statements of the staff of the University of Minnesota–Twin Cities Office of Admissions is:

CHIEF OF STAFF:

◀ Keep the office on track for success.

◀ Ensure the office's major, "high stakes" projects are successful.

ASSISTANT DIRECTOR OF FRESHMAN ADMISSIONS:

◀ Shape the class according to University's expectations.

◀ Ensure fair, consistent, timely, cost-effective admission decisions.

Web-Based Application for Office of Admissions

The Tri-O management operating system also requires that an effective mission statement be developed for each major project and activity.

When the Office of Admissions decided to work with an outside vendor to develop and implement a new web-based application for admission, our Chief of Staff managed the project for our office and established the following mission statement for the project: "Friendly and Flawless." Our Chief of Staff made it clear to all of the persons involved in developing the new web-based application for admission that these words meant:

◀ **"Friendly"**—Highly user-oriented. The new application must meet the needs of the Office of Admissions and the University to collect key data, but be designed to encourage a prospective student to complete the application. We cannot admit and enroll a prospect unless we have a complete application on file.

◀ **"Flawless"**—There was no margin for error since the application was being brought online in the middle of the application season to replace another web-based application for admission. Design, programming, or implementation flaws could be extremely serious for the University, so a zero tolerance for problems was established.

These three simple words provided the clear guidance that led to a very successful development and implementation of the new online application. Everyone involved in the project clearly knew what the project's expected outcomes were. The new web application resulted in 71 percent of freshman applicants applying via the Web for fall 2006 versus 48 percent for fall 2005.

University of Minnesota Office of Counseling & Consultative Services

I recently walked to a meeting on campus and passed by the building where the University's Office of Counseling & Consultative Services is located. Outside the building they had a sign placed next to the sidewalk that read:

> *University Counseling & Consultative Services Can Help You*
> * *Improve grades*
> * *Choose a major*
> * *Tackle personal problems*
>
> *Come on In!*

This may not be the exact office mission statement for the University's Office of Counseling & Consultative Services, but it certainly could be because it's a wonderful example of an office that effectively translated the services that it offers into benefits that can be clearly understood by its potential customers.

Developing an Effective Tri-O Outcome-Oriented Mission Statement

There are four steps in the process of developing an outcome-oriented mission statement:

◀ **Step One:** Identify the major functions and duties of your organization or your program. Some of the functions and duties will be more indicative of stakeholder expectations than others. However, most were derived from stakeholder expectations at some point in time.

◀ **Step Two:** List the major stakeholders for your program.

◀ **Step Three:** Define how your organization's or program's stakeholders define success for your organization, i.e., the outcomes they value and expect from your organization.

◀ **Step Four:** Develop a five to 15 word mission statement for your organization describing what outcomes your organization or unit will consistently deliver for its stakeholders.

Process-Oriented versus Outcomes-Oriented Mission Statements

Table 5.1 lists several examples of program or unit mission statements that are process-oriented and their transformation into outcome-oriented mission statements. All of the examples are hypothetical.

Table 5.1. *Process-Oriented vs. Outcome-Oriented Program or Unit Mission Statements*

ORGANIZATION/ UNIT	PROCESS-ORIENTED	OUTCOME-ORIENTED
Academic Advising	◀ Provide outstanding academic advising to enrolled students ◀ Meet once a term with advisees ◀ Keep student records updated	◀ Advisees graduate in four years ◀ X % of freshman advisees return to the institution as sophomores
Career Planning & Placement	◀ Provide outstanding career planning & placement services to enrolled students and alumni	◀ X % of graduates find a job related to their interests within X months of graduation
One-Stop Student Services Office	◀ Respond to student inquiries in a timely fashion with accurate information	◀ Begin to respond to each inquiry within 30 seconds of receipt of call ◀ Make it easy for students to do business with the University ◀ Provide standard information to students even before they ask for it.
Financial Aid Offices	◀ Distribute financial aid in a timely fashion	◀ Directly impact recruitment, retention and four-year graduation rate

Table 5.2 lists several examples of project mission statements.

Table 5.2. *Process-Oriented vs. Outcome-Oriented Project Mission Statements*

PROJECT	PROCESS-ORIENTED	OUTCOME-ORIENTED
Online application for admission	◀ Collaborate with key colleagues on campus to produce the application ◀ Make it easy for prospective students to apply ◀ A process that works without problems for the applicant and the institution	◀ Friendly and flawless
Prospective student open house	◀ Hold an open house on X date for prospective students and their parents	◀ Open house on X date ◀ At least X number of high school junior prospects and their parents attend

It's Well Worth the Effort!

An effective mission statement must be developed for each program in the organization. Ideally, each person in the organization should also develop a mission statement. At a minimum, it is imperative that persons with managerial responsibilities develop personal mission statements. Also, mission statements must be developed for each major project to ensure the achievement of specific outcomes.

Taking the time to develop an effective mission statement for your organization is well worth the effort. It's the key to determining where the organization is headed and what it plans to accomplish.

....
CASE STUDY 8:
WHAT HAPPENS WHEN AN ORGANIZATION'S
MISSION MAY NO LONGER BE RELEVANT

LESSONS
FOR HIGHER
EDUCATION
MANAGERS

The most dangerous time is when an organization is at the top of its game. It's easy to bask in success and "stick with what brought us here."

All organizations must continually evolve or risk becoming
irrelevant. Companies that do not evolve with the marketplace are either weakened or eliminated by the competition.

There is currently considerable discussion in the business-related press about the need for business schools to redefine their missions to better serve their students and the businesses and organizations that ultimately hire their graduates.

Warren G. Bennis and James O'Toole, business professors at the University of Southern California, argue that business schools have lost their way. The following are excerpts from their May 2005 *Harvard Business Review* article.

Business schools are on the wrong track. For many years, MBA pro-grams enjoyed rising respectability in academia and growing prestige in the business world. Their admissions were ever more selective, the pay packages of graduates ever more dazzling. Today, however, MBA programs face intense criticism for failing to impart useful skills, fail-ing to prepare leaders, failing to instill norms of ethical behavior—and even failing to lead graduates to good corporate jobs. These criticisms come not just from students, employers, and the media but also from deans of some of America's most prestigious business schools....

The actual cause of today's crisis in management education is far broader in scope and can be traced to a dramatic shift in the culture of business schools. During the past several decades, many leading B schools have quietly adopted an inappropriate—and ultimately self-defeating—model of academic excellence. Instead of measuring them-selves in terms of the competence of their graduates, or by how well their faculties understand important drivers of business performance, they measure themselves almost solely by the rigor of their scientific research. They have adopted a model of science that uses abstract financial and economic analysis, statistical multiple regressions, and

laboratory psychology. Some of the research produced is excellent,
but because so little of it is grounded in actual business practices, the
focus of graduate business education has become increasingly circum-
scribed- and less and less relevant to practitioners.

Bennis and O'Toole (2005) point out that "Today it is possible
to find tenured professors of management who have never set foot
inside a real business, except as customers."

They offer a number of suggestions for making the curriculum of
today's business schools more relevant. They hold that:

> *The problem is not that business schools have embraced scientific*
> *rigor but that they have forsaken other forms of knowledge.... It isn't*
> *a case of either-or...In practice, business schools need a diverse faculty*
> *populated with professors who, collectively, hold a variety of skills and*
> *interests that cover territory as broad and as deep as business itself.*

Not surprisingly, there are many other views on how to make
today's business schools more relevant. Some observers, such as USC
business school professors Harry and Linda DeAngelo and University
of Rochester business professor Jerold Zimmerman, maintain that,
"...the hiring and promotion of research faculty—is an unqualified
success story, transforming B-schools from glorified trade schools
into truly academic institutions" (Lavelle 2005).

The DeAngelos and Zimmerman

> *...lay the blame for B-schools' woes squarely at the doorstep of*
> *media rankings—like those produced by Business Week—and the B-*
> *school deans who pander to them. The authors maintain that U.S.*
> *business schools are in thrall to the rankings, so much so that they're*
> *abandoning the 'rigorous conceptual framework' that students need in*
> *favor of 'quick fixes' to improve their place in the rankings but do little*
> *to help students.* (Lavelle 2005)

The active dialogue and sometimes strong disagreement regarding
the mission and curricula of today's business schools is very healthy.
In fact, this process is necessary for business schools to continue to

change and improve. If, however, a particular business school cannot reach a workable consensus on its mission, it can be a serious problem for the organization. Lack of a relatively clear mission can lead to a dysfunctional organization and the failure to achieve meaningful outcomes and real excellence. The differences must be resolved so that the mission of a particular business school can be made operational by the majority of its faculty and staff.

Case
Study

CASE STUDY 9:
CLEARLY UNDERSTANDING THE MISSION

LESSONS
FOR HIGHER
EDUCATION
MANAGERS

It's fine to have a team full of superstars, but you won't win unless everyone can and will play a specific role in the project instead of seeking their own personal glory.

A team of superstars simply cannot win without teamwork.

An absolutely wonderful example of the importance of the members of an organization fully understanding their mission and the role they play in achieving the mission was the Discovery Channel Cycling Team's success in helping Lance Armstrong achieve a record setting seventh win in the 2005 Tour de France. The world famous grueling bike race is run in 21 stages over an almost consecutive three-week period.

Team member George Hincapie was fourth in the second day's time trials. Achieving this excellent result was not new for Hincapie who is a highly accomplished cyclist in his own right. The following excerpts from Samuel Abt's (2005) article following the second day's time trials, illustrate Hincapie's clear understanding and acceptance of his mission in helping Lance Armstrong win his seventh Tour de France:

[Hincapie] is the only rider who has been with Armstrong in all six of his Tour victories, during which the Texan has won 21 daily stages and his teammates none.

...Hincapie will be in his usual role of a mainstay support rider, devoted not to his own welfare but to keeping his team leader in position to win again.

After the opening time trial, Hincapie said... "*My job is only a question of staying with Lance and protecting him. I'll keep him out of the wind and away from dangerous riders, the kind of guys who cause crashes. I'll chase down breakaways and set a pace early in the mountains."*

Hincapie noted that… "The whole point is to try to have him (Armstrong) do as little work as possible, to let him save his energy, until it's time for him to start winning."

Hincapie…delights in his selfless role. "It's hard work, but very fulfilling," he said. "I wouldn't trade my part for anything."

"The team is built around one person, Lance," Hincapie said. "It's a big honor to help him win year after year. We've been creating history."

Now with his sparkling fourth place in the time trial, he will bury any longing for individual success until the one-day classics resume in August.

"It's not a sacrifice," he insisted, "I definitely could go for stage victories if I were riding for another team, but it's more important to be part of making history.

"This is Lance's last year, but it's not mine. I've got years ahead of me to try to win for myself."

It's clear that it takes both outstanding talent and dedication to win a highly demanding event such as the Tour de France. It also takes effective strategy and teamwork to win. Each member of the team, from the cyclist, team sponsor, and manager to the support group, must clearly understand the overall mission of the team and how each team member must make his or her own unique contributions to achieving the overall goal.

George Hincapie demonstrated both his clear understanding of the team's mission and his individual mission. This approach by the entire Discovery Channel Cycling Team, combined with talent and dedication, contributed to Lance Armstrong winning the prestigious 2005 Tour de France.

CASE STUDY 10:
BEING CLEAR ON EXPECTED OUTCOMES

LESSONS
FOR HIGHER
EDUCATION
MANAGERS

Activity, even by brilliant people, is not sufficient for success. The activities must be focused on outcomes and not just interesting and hard work.

Neal Gendler's (2005) article about George Buckley, the person who became the CEO of the 3M Corporation in 2005, illustrates the importance of understanding an organization or a unit's mission. The following are excerpts from the article.

> *Buckley indicated that he "…intends to give some latitude to scientists and engineers to develop pet ideas, some of which have led to spectacular successes such as Post-it Notes….Buckley made clear, though, that he expects research and development to have a payoff.*
>
> *"3M has a magnificent history of (research and development), but in the end, the mission of 'R&D' is to turn those investment dollars into products. You empower people to do things, you give them something, but they have to give something back," he said.*
>
> *Buckley noted that "[M]anagement's duty is to 'make sure they're working on things that might have the chance to come to fruition.'"*

6

PURPOSE

Empowers an
organization's people to
stay on track for success

OUTCOMES

Effective staff
development program

Effective, workable
staff performance
evaluation process

Tri-O

STAR TRACKER
COMPONENT

Who is the best coach?
The one with the best talent.

~ BUM PHILLIPS (1991)

An organization's people are its most precious resource. The comment by "Bum" Phillips, once head coach of the former Houston Oilers professional football team, reinforces this reality.

A *New York Times* article emphasizes the importance of recruiting top talent. The article points out that Bobby Gonzalez had been hired as the new basketball coach at Seton Hall, as well as Fred Hill at Rutgers, and Barry Rohrssen at Manhattan, in part, because of their ability to recruit, especially in their own backyards. Bobby Gonzalez, the new Seton Hall coach made this observation:

> *"The business has changed, and the reason it has changed is people realize that guys who are good coaches but can't recruit won't last very long," Gonzalez said. "If a guy is a great recruiter and no better than a solid coach, he will survive. That's because in this business*

CHAPTER 6 *Tri-O Star Tracker Component*

there is so much emphasis on getting players. If you can't get players, you've got no chance." (Finley 2006)

The Tri-O Star Tracker empowers an organization's people to stay on track for success. This component is called "Star Tracker" to reflect the importance of our people to our organization. We recognize that we have a lot of great people working with us and we want to empower them to use their talents and recognize their contributions to the success of our program.

I noted in Chapter 4, "The Tri-O Compass," John Kotter's observation that an effective organization must recognize the difference between leadership and management and make certain that its managers and staff collectively develop and implement both sets of skills (*see* page 53). Tri-O is termed a Management Operating System, but again, "management" is a catch-all shorthand for a comprehensive operating system that helps ensure that both leadership and management skills are consistently implemented.

A Work-in-Progress

In the early chapters of this book, I explained that Tri-O is both a working and an aspirational system. The Tri-O Star Tracker component is the most "work-in-progress" of the seven Tri-O components. Some days we seem right on target with the leadership and management of our office. Other days, I am painfully aware that we need to make significant improvements in both areas. This probably reflects both my strengths and weaknesses as a leader. It also reflects the reality that leadership is a highly demanding task and that all of us, to some degree, constantly struggle with trying to be effective.

We are a sum total of our genetics, education, training, and experiences. The early role models to which I was exposed often reflected a hierarchal, top-down, serious approach to leadership and management. I grew up in a strong family that applied a patriarchal and Calvinist model to life. While I revere to this day the people who taught and mentored me over the years in my church, I have come to realize the extent to which it employed, in those days, a hierarchal, literal, rules-oriented approach. When I moved into the work environment, many of my supervisors practiced a command and control mode which is essentially characterized by the top leaders telling the rest of the organization what things to do and how to do it. Therefore, for a significant portion of my professional career, I employed what I knew—a hierarchical command and control model.

I really admire the people that I have worked with over the years that seem to be "naturals" at both good leadership and management. They can make certain that their organization meets its goals for outcomes while maintaining high morale. However, these natural leaders are very much the exception rather then the rule. Most of the leaders with whom I have worked have tended to be too tough or too lenient. I believe that most managers struggle to find an appropriate balance between these two ends of the spectrum.

As I have had substantial academic training in leadership and management, read extensively on my own in these subjects, and held leadership positions at work and in organizations, my views of leadership and management have evolved. While I knew that I did not flourish in a work environment that emphasized a rigid top-down, hierarchical, command and control approach, that was the only model I knew; that was my paradigm.

I firmly believe that to be successful, managers must engage both the heads and hearts of their organization's people. The head or cognitive aspect is crucial to gaining people's acceptance of one's leadership through logic and experience. However, the heart is as essential as the head. Without engaging people's passion and real commitment, an organization will never be truly great.

I have seen many managers fail to fully develop an organization because they have ultimate faith in their intelligence and rational skills, yet fail to recognize that they must also engage people's hearts in the enterprise.

For further reading on this topic, I recommend that you read *Encouraging the Heart, A Leader's Guide to Rewarding and Recognizing Others*, by James M. Kouzes and Barry Z. Posner (1999).

The Tri-O system may not be the perfect Management Operating System. It is, however, a *working* system that has helped my institution to be very successful with its undergraduate enrollment.

CHAPTER 6 *Tri-O Star Tracker Component*

90

Over-Managed and Under-Led

In a 1990 *Harvard Business Review* article, "What Leaders Really Do," John P. Kotter observed that:

> *Most U.S. corporations today are overmanaged and underled. They need to develop their capacity to exercise leadership. Successful corporations don't wait for leaders to come along. They actively seek out people with leadership potential and expose them to career experiences designed to develop that potential. Indeed, with careful selection, nurturing, and encouragement, dozens of people can play important leadership roles in a business organization.*

Kotter's 1990 observation about the corporate world is applicable today to the nation's colleges and universities—many are over-managed and under-led. However, during my years in higher education, I have witnessed major strides forward in the both the leadership and management of colleges and universities.

Like the corporate world, much of higher education is now devoting significant resources to the development of leaders at all levels of the organization. This is based on the recognition that its people are valuable resources that must be developed and retained because the success of the organization is directly tied to the success of it people. Also, colleges and universities are increasingly recognizing that as faculty and staff move progressively through the leadership ranks, they are not finished products and need continued development.

There is, however, still a lot of work to do. My views and understanding of this are influenced in recent years by the researchers of the concept of emotional intelligence, which is featured later in this chapter and its case study section.

Many higher education managers have long excelled in the intellectual aspects of their work but often are not good at inspiring the troops. I view this as a failure to balance the head and heart.

Leadership

A high degree of intelligence is valued in higher education. Indeed, many of the smartest people on earth work in colleges and universities. I have seen major growth in the vision, planning, and budgeting aspects of higher education leadership, perhaps because these tasks are enhanced by the cognitive strength of its managers.

However, as discovered by the researchers of emotional intelligence, intelligence alone is not sufficient for success in leadership and management positions. Effective development of the non-cognitive or affective side of leadership is also crucial. I have witnessed that this is still lacking in many managers and leaders in higher education at all levels. I find that most higher education managers are well-meaning, honorable, and kind people. However, they are either not trained in, or are simply indifferent to, the importance of a balance between the cognitive and the "human" side of management.

Many managers may gain the attention of their staff's heads but they often fail to also engage their hearts. The result is good work from their troops without providing an atmosphere that encourages optimal work. An undue emphasis on management over leadership can literally cut the heart out of an organization and its people. Most people want to do a great job. They simply need to know how their work contributes to the greater good of the organization and that they and their work are respected, and they must work in an atmosphere that brings out and rewards their best ideas and efforts.

Political skills are important in securing and remaining in leadership positions. Higher education leaders that are consistently successful are skilled in this important area. However, political skills are only a portion of the human side of management. Many higher education leaders are either one or two trick ponies in respect to their approach to leadership, and emphasize too much either the "carrot" or the "stick" aspects of motivation and generally err on the side of the "stick" and the authority bestowed by their titles.

Management

Higher education managers often fall short as effective managers because they have not taken time to develop a personal mission statement. Failing to take time to identify which roles are primarily strategic and which are primarily tactical, causes many to micromanage when they should be working primarily at the strategic level.

Some managers are not effective delegators who could bene-fit from the guidelines outlined in Chapter 8, "Tri-O Delegation Component," on page 135.

The Implications of Emotional Intelligence on Leadership and Management

It would be extremely worthwhile for every higher education man-ager to spend time studying the concept of emotional intelligence. Several pages of this book provide a brief overview of emotional intelligence and its implications for our work as higher education managers. I believe the work of researchers and writers who focus on emotional intelligence is especially relevant to this discussion on managing for outcomes.

Cary Cherniss (2000) notes that the term "emotional intelligence" was coined by Salovey and Mayer in 1990—

> *They described emotional intelligence as a "form of social intelli-gence that involves the ability to monitor one's own and others' feelings and emotions, to discriminate among them, and to use this informa-tion to guide one's thinking and action."*
>
> *Ever since the publication of Daniel Goleman's first book on the topic in 1995, emotional intelligence has become one of the hottest buzzwords in corporate America. For instance, when the Harvard Business Review published an article on the topic two years ago, it attracted a higher percentage of readers than any other article pub-lished in that periodical in the last 40 years....*

No "silver bullet" will address all situations, especially with some-thing as complex as dealing with people. Nonetheless, time spent studying this concept and its implications for leadership and manage-ment would be time very well spent by higher education managers.

Case Study numbers 11, 12 and 13 provide additional insight into the importance of emotional intelligence to success as a leader and manager.

What is Leadership?

In his March-April 2000 *Harvard Business Review* article, "Leadership That Gets Results," Daniel Goleman (2000) starts this article with the following:

> *Ask any group of businesspeople the question "What do effective leaders do?" and you'll hear a sweep of answers. Leaders set strategy; they motivate; they create a mission; they build a culture. Then ask, "What **should** leaders do?" If the group is seasoned, you'll likely hear one response: the leader's singular job is to get results.*

There are perhaps hundreds of definitions of leadership. I believe that a column in *USA Today* by Gladys Edmunds does an excellent job of outlining what defines leadership in an era in which an organization must clearly recognize that outcomes are produced by the organization's people—it's most precious resource.

Excerpts of Ms. Edmund's (2006) column, "Leadership isn't a popularity contest" are included below:

> *There are many aspects to leadership, but popularity is not one of them. Think of the many popular people you know. You will see that many can be the life of the party but are not necessarily the leader of the pack.*
>
> *Leadership is all about getting results and meeting goals and objectives.*
>
> *As you think about who might be a good fit to place at the head of your company, think about some of the following things:*
>
> ⋆ *A good leader, no matter what the situation or age, puts time and effort into self-improvement. They take pride in all aspects of their life. And, they set standards by doing and not just delegating.*
>
> ⋆ *Leaders are able to motivate people to work together in order to achieve results. They encourage teamwork in order to meet objectives and goals.*
>
> ⋆ *Leaders are good communicators. They speak well and listen intently, and they know the difference between the two and how to use both effectively.*
>
> ⋆ *Leaders set examples and don't shy away from problems. They help bring out the best in their employees and give them a sense of*

*self-worth. As Catherine the Great once said, "Good leaders praise
loudly and blame softly."*

Three Pillars of the Tri-O Star Tracker Component

Because an organization's people are its most precious resource, it is
important to select outstanding people and then help them continue
to develop. Therefore, the Star Tracker Component rests on three
primary pillars:

◀ Staff Selection and Development
◀ Staff Performance Assessment
◀ Rewarding and Recognizing Staff

Staff Selection and Development

In the admissions program at Minnesota we spend a lot of time both
selecting our staff and training and developing them.

Staff Selection: Building a Team Based on What People Can Do

In his outstanding book, *Managing the Nonprofit Organization,
Principals and Practices*, Peter F. Drucker (1990) provides valuable
advice on staff selection and developing people. The following are
excerpts from Drucker's chapter on "People Decisions:"

> *...[O]ne doesn't try to build on people's weaknesses...*
>
> *... By the time people come to work, their personalities are set. One
> can expect adults to develop manners and behavior and to learn skills
> and knowledge. But one has to use people's personalities the way they
> are, not the way we would like them to be...*
>
> *... Don't hire a person for what they can't do, hire them for what
> they can do.*
>
> *...The lesson is to focus on strengths...Then make really stringent
> demands, and take the time and trouble (it's hard work) to review
> performance. Sit down with people and say: This is what you and I
> committed ourselves to a year ago. How have you done? What have
> you done well?....*
>
> *...A common mistake is to believe that because individuals are all
> on the same team, they all think alike and act alike. Not so. The pur-
> pose of a team is to make the strengths of each person effective, and*

his or her weaknesses irrelevant. One manages individuals on a team. The focus is to look at the performance and the strengths of individuals combined in joint effort.

It has taken me a long time to fully operationalize Drucker's observations in staff selection and staff development for the programs with which I work. This lesson was driven home to me as I worked with Merit Scholars[4] over the years. At various times in my career, I have personally involved myself in the recruitment of these top prospects. The recruitment process involved getting to know the prospects and their families very well. When they enrolled at my institution, they often felt comfortable in stopping by my office to ask for advice. Seeing the personal growth of students has been a very rewarding process for me personally because I love working with students.

Almost invariably, a number of the newly enrolled Merit Scholars would stop by my office and observe that they were having trouble with a specific course during their first or second semester in college. The course involved would vary from student to student but what transcended all of the conversations was the realization that, for what may be the first time in their academic careers, they were having difficulty with a subject. I found myself assuring them that although they are among the most capable students in the country, they have strengths and weakness like everyone else. I assured them that they were not inadequate or a failure because of their difficulty with a course, and that it is simply part of the educational and developmental process at the college level.

As I can now better assess my own strengths and weaknesses, I am better able to understand the real wisdom of Drucker's observation. I realize that if I am going to consistently achieve the outcomes specified in my personal mission statement (discussed in Chapter 5, on page 65), then I must focus on the things that I can do well, improve on the things I do not do as well (but cannot delegate), and ask team members to focus on their strengths to offset my weaknesses. I am now confident enough in myself to admit that I cannot do some

---

[4] Merit Scholarship is a trademark of the National Merit Scholarship Corporation

96

things as well as others, and should ask them to take on those responsibilities. It has been a long journey for me.

Case Study #14: "Why Dream Teams Fail," on page 109, emphasizes that talent alone will not ensure success; it must be blended into effective teamwork.

Staff Development

◀ **Staffing Depth Charts:** It is common for athletic coaches to maintain a chart that lists the starter and back-ups for each position on the team. The chart enables the coaches to gain a quick assessment of positions where they are thin in staffing and provides a means to plan for recruiting and developing future players.

We maintain an informal staffing depth chart in the Office of Admissions at Minnesota for the same purposes. First, we want to make certain that we have back-ups in place in the event of promotions, vacations, extended absences from the office or staff leaving for other positions. Additionally, we want to look one and two years ahead in respect to our staffing needs so we can make certain that we, when appropriate, are developing in-house talent to consider for vacant or new positions.

Since our people are our most precious resource, developing talent is one of the most important jobs of our senior managers. This is an area where we especially seek to be proactive rather than play defense.

◀ **Communicate! Communicate! Communicate!** Our staff is among our managers' major internal stakeholders. Therefore, we hold frequent staff meetings to communicate directly with them and to listen to their concerns and suggestions. Effective staff meetings are an important team-building tool and a way to calibrate an organization's mission and values with the staff. I recognize that some staff meetings can be unproductive and we work to remedy this where needed. However, I strongly believe that it is important to Communicate! Communicate! Communicate!

◀ **Planned Staff Turnover:** We seek and plan for appropriate turnover in our entry-level professional staff. On the surface this may seem harsh. However, in reality, it is kinder to the staff member, their peers, and the entire program.

The admissions counselor position is, for the most part, the entry-level professional staff position in our office. We offer our new admissions counselors a one-year contract with the expectation that they can stay in this entry-level position for a maximum of three years. We then expect them to either seek to move up in our office or at the University, move to another position outside our office, or move onto graduate or professional school.

While there are definite and valid exceptions to this rule, we generally do not want our professional staff to stay in an entry-level position for an inordinate amount of time. We find that if this happens, human nature often takes over. After we are in a position for some time, we identify what we like and do not like to do. We then often try to reposition our duties to focus on what we like to do. While this is natural, it causes problems for an office because there are certain basic duties that absolutely must be done. While we ensure that these duties are completed, we try to offer new staff opportunities for professional growth and very much try to retain our best performers.

◀ **The Importance of Peer Leadership:** Staff at all levels of an organization has duties that require the skillful application of leadership skills. Persons with supervisory titles should clearly understand this responsibility. However, some of the most effective leaders in an organization do not have a leadership role reflected in their titles, but are, in practice, leaders.

Copying successful sports teams, the University of Minnesota Office of Admissions stresses the development of "team captains." Captains can, at times, have more credibility and influence than some of the more "official" leaders. The team captains are peer leaders who are expected, for example, to help their peers (especially newcomers) understand the culture of the office and set a positive and productive tone for the office. You generally cannot advance in the official leadership structure of the Office of Admissions unless you have demonstrated the ability and willingness to be an effective "team captain."

CHAPTER 6 *Tri-O Star Tracker Component*

I will cite just one of many impressive peer leadership activities. One of our Admissions Counselors is very talented in using his computer to design photo collage posters. He often makes a poster to welcome new staff members to his unit. He also welcomes back staff from a long vacation or leave of absence with a specially designed poster. This "little" touch is a wonderful way to help build a real team.

◀ **Tri-O Management Academy:** The University of Minnesota offers its full-time employees an opportunity to take courses at the University with the tuition paid by the University's Regents Scholarship Program. We also send our staff to relevant courses offered through our campus Department of Human Resources. and encourage them to attend conferences that will increase their understanding of the profession and enhance their skills. We especially encourage our staff to be presenters at conferences and to seek leadership positions in professional organizations to further develop their leadership and professional skills

As an additional way to develop our management talent and to instill the Tri-O system throughout the culture of the Office of Admissions, we will soon start our own "Tri-O Management Academy." We have already held intensive Tri-O training for our senior managers. We are now incorporating formal Tri-O training into all managerial and operational levels of our office.

We have also conducted mini-seminars on Tri-O for several of the college-based student services units on the Twin Cities campus and offer the more intensive Tri-O training to interested managers on campus.

◀ **Student Employees:** Colleges and universities are the beneficiaries of an especially rich pool of talent—their students. Most colleges and universities rely heavily on students to help with their work. Many student employees have amazing skills and talents. (Of course, they are our students!) The only thing some of them lack is experience, and they are often just a semester or two away from earning their bachelor's degrees and "certifications" as "real" professionals. Several of the top managers in the Minnesota Office of

Admissions began their career here as student assistants or volunteers in our office.

In the Minnesota Office of Admissions we work hard to include our student assistants in our "family." Many of our students work with us for all four years of their undergraduate work and recommend their brothers and sisters to us. Our student assistants are part of many of our office-wide and unit celebrations. We provide opportunities for our very best student employees to move into student supervisory positions in our office. We also offer several undergraduate internships to enable students to start building a professional resumé and portfolio.

It is a source of personal satisfaction for our staff to watch new student employees, many of whom are inexperienced and shy, turn into confident, outstanding young adults four years later.

◀ **Volunteers:** Like most nonprofit organizations, colleges and universities depend on the involvement of volunteers in their work. The Minnesota Office of Admissions is no exception. The University and our office greatly benefits from the wonderful contributions of student, parent, and alumni volunteers.

There are several keys to the successful involvement of volunteers in the work of a college or university:

◀ Set clear expectations for outcomes, and the boundaries of their involvement.

◀ Respect their time and expertise. Ask them to serve in ways that respect their very busy schedules and use their special skills and talents.

◀ Recognize them for their contributions.

◀ Make certain their work is coordinated by a staff member. There is no such thing as absolutely "free" volunteer assistance. Like any worthwhile endeavor, volunteer programs require effective leadership and nurturing.

Rewarding and Recognizing Staff

We reward and recognize staff in the Minnesota Office of Admissions in various ways. I am not as creative or risk-taking as some of our staff on this matter, so I often rely on them to lead us in this area.

Some ways to reward staff are office-wide efforts and some are unique to a particular unit based on the creativity of that unit's manager. The basic premise behind these efforts is to recognize and encourage outstanding performance. We understand that we cannot expect our staff to be loyal unless we are loyal to them.

◀ **Salaries:** Money is not the only thing that motivates staff, but it is very important. We, of course, follow the University's regulations and guidelines for staff compensation. We also do not have unlimited funds for staff salaries and raises. However, since we expect a lot from our staff, we do our best to pay our staff salaries very competitively with their peers around the country. We do not skimp in this critical area!

◀ **Flex-Time:** We try to use flexible schedules, or flex time, as appropriate and reasonable to acknowledge a particular staff member's personal or family circumstances. The key to making it work is that the expected outcomes must be clearly stated and accomplished.

◀ **Casual Days:** Our office expects staff working in public contact positions to dress in a professional fashion. Our freshman admissions unit has found allowing its staff to dress casually on specified days or weeks when they are not in the public eye is a much appreciated stress reducer. Even on days when staff are on public contact duty, occasionally a supervisor will declare a casual day to celebrate a certain percentage of staff contributing to a worthy charity; these casual days are announced to our guests.

◀ **Movie Days:** Our freshman admissions unit will occasionally call a special afternoon "staff meeting" and then instead of an actual meeting, the supervisors will send the staff to a movie at office expense. The supervisors keep the office running while the staff is at the movies. This is an especially good stress reliever during times of peak workload.

Also, some our units will hold a movie and pizza night in our office auditorium to reward student assistants for outstanding performance.

◀ **Staff Celebrations:** We hold periodic office-wide celebrations, most often with food. Often these are very informal occasions. Karaoke seems to be a staff favorite, especially when managers like me are willing to display their lack of singing ability.

At times of high stress, we will periodically send out a surprise e-mail to our entire staff announcing that there are bagels, cookies, or a variety of pies in the break areas. We make certain that our student assistants are included in these celebrations since they are an integral and valuable part of our staff.

We believe that it is especially important to serve items that our staff will recognize as quality products such as Mrs. Fields cookies or Baker's Square pies. Since we expect the best from our staff we must also recognize that they are the best. It is also important to have an adequate supply of food available so each person can eat, within limits, as much as they want. Because our staff is generous with their time and contributions, we want the quality and quantity of food to convey generosity in return.

We do not have unlimited funds and we are a taxpayer-supported institution. Therefore, we are very careful to only do things that we could defend to the people of Minnesota. I will sometimes supplement our funds for these activities by donating an honorarium or consulting fee to the office discretionary fund.

◀ **The "M" Pin:** Several years ago we opened a new visitors' center in our office. Just outside the visitors' center, a large University of Minnesota "M" sign with "Admissions" printed across it was installed. The architects had designed the sign as an attention grabber to direct visitors to our office.

We had an office event to celebrate the opening of the new visitors' center. One of our Associate Directors, who is especially wonderful in building teams, had a small (inexpensive) pin designed and produced to replicate the very classy sign outside our visitors' center. At the office event, we gave each of our staff a pin and we now give each new staff a pin during an office-wide ceremony.

I firmly believe that the Office of Admissions is the very best administrative unit on campus, an assumption that I suspect many of our fine colleagues around campus would take exception to! We want our staff to take pride in and have a strut in their step because of their consistently outstanding performance. The "M" pin has come to symbolize membership in a top-notch administrative unit that takes pride in its accomplishments.

Staff Performance Assessment

Key Assumptions of the Star Tracker
(Performance Evaluation) Assessment Process:

◀ **A management operating system is only as good as the people managing and implementing it.** Tri-O is stakeholder-focused and outcome-oriented. Ultimately, an organization's people achieve the outcomes. Because people are an organization's most valuable resource, the Tri-O Star Tracker System assumes that an organization will hire, coach, and reward the best talent available.

◀ **Most people want to be successful.** While some staff may perform more effectively than others, most people want to do a good job and take pride in their work. There are often various staff-related factors that influence performance, and the management literature is filled with opinions and research in this area. Many external factors outside the staff member's influence can also impact a person's contribution to the office. The Tri-O system helps alleviate some of the external barriers to outstanding achievement by providing the leadership and management tools necessary to focus on the achievement of success.

◀ **People perform better when the goals and expectations are clear.** While there is a certain amount of stress associated with knowing that you are responsible for achieving specific outcomes, not knowing what is expected is even more stressful. Employees cannot meet performance expectations if expectations are not clear. Allowing employees to perform at a mediocre level by not providing clear expectations is unfair to them and to the organization.

◀ **The Tri-O management game plan is positive and achievement-oriented, rather than punitive in nature.** The sign on a Houston, Texas church once read: *"There is no reward in finding fault."*

The Tri-O system is predicated on clear definitions of success, with components in place to help ensure success. No one wins with negativity and faultfinding. Everyone wins when the focus is on achievement.

◀ **The discussion about expectations and performance is a year-long activity.** An annual performance review can cause undue stress. Often, it is the only time employees learn how their supervisor has assessed their performance. The entire Tri-O system is based on frequent and ongoing candid conversations. By holding frequent outcome-oriented discussions, the employee and supervisor are able to focus on what needs to be accomplished rather than viewing such conversations as a faultfinding call to accountability. Key Success Indicators (KSIs), outlined in Chapter 10 on page 174, are one of the major Tri-O tools to encourage frequent performance discussions.

I believe in what is often called the "management by walking around" approach. I prefer to have frequent informal and short discussions with our managers to make certain that we are on the same page about outcome expectations.

The Tri-O Star Tracker Performance Assessment Form

Like many programs around the country, we have struggled to develop the "perfect" performance evaluation instrument.

Several years ago, the admissions staff at Minnesota determined that the University's performance evaluation form did not fit the culture of this office. We assembled a committee to develop one that matched the outcome-oriented nature of the office and to encourage dialogue between managers and staff. During the development process, the committee consulted extensively with the admissions staff, the University's Office of Human Resources, and representatives of the University's Civil Service Committee. The office adopted a single form that is used by our union, civil service, and professional and administrative staff.

Our evaluation form, however, is still a work-in-progress and continues to be modified based on our experience. Our current thinking on this process is to essentially ask our managers to address, with each of their staff, the items that are listed in Figure 6.1, "The Star Tracker Performance Evaluation Form," on page 104.

The completion of a performance evaluation form on an annual basis is not an end unto itself, but rather another opportunity to have a productive, positive conversation about where the office is headed and how each of us can contribute to the achievement of the office's goals.

Conditions Supportive of Organizational Success

I sat one weekend afternoon in a coffee shop in Dinkytown, just off the Minnesota campus, and made a list of what best helps me personally be content and productive in an organization. My rationale for developing this list was to consider successful, adequate, and poor organizational conditions at the colleges and universities and programs with which I have worked over the years.

Figure 6.2 contains a list of the conditions that I think should exist in an organization that wants to have high productivity, as measured by outcomes, and high morale.

To some degree, this list may represent my view of organizational utopia. I cannot say that all of these conditions exist in the Office of Admissions at Minnesota, but we are working toward it.

> **Figure 6.1.** *The Star Tracker Performance Evaluation Form*
>
> **SELF ASSESSMENT**
> ◀ Assess your job performance for the current review period. Comment on each of the following areas: (a) achievements or performance highlights; (b) goals met.
> ◀ State any unmet goals and comment on your performance related to them.
> ◀ Comment on areas needing improvement and areas where you wish to develop new skill sets.
> ◀ State your goals for next year.
>
> **EVALUATION BY SUPERVISOR**
> ◀ Comment on employee's job performance, achievements and highlights, and goals met for the current review period.
> ◀ Comment on unmet goals and related performance issues, as well as areas needing improvement.
> ◀ State employee's goals for next year.

Flowers for the Living

I have often been struck by the importance of recognizing colleagues who pass away or who retire after effective service at an organization. It is fitting to respect and remember people at such times. At the same time, I believe it is very important to acknowledge people during the high points, low points, and every day of their career. I believe that we all need to be acknowledged and encouraged.

I was deeply affected at the graveside service for my mother on the Eastern Shore of Maryland when I saw a bouquet of flowers sent by the Admissions Staff back home in Houston, Texas. It was sent in respect for my wonderful and honorable mother. It deeply touched my heart as one of the living. I have never forgotten this act of kindness from the Houston folks because I personally found that what may be a tradition at times of sadness can also be a meaningful and personal act of encouragement.

Figure 6.2. *Key Ingredients for High Productivity and Morale*

◀ Ethics and honor
◀ Meeting stakeholder expectations by 1) treating the organization's people with genuine respect, and 2) providing a caring, collaborative, supportive environment.
◀ Clear expectations and dialogue about what each individual must achieve and a clear understanding that outcomes are not optional.
◀ Mediocrity and failure is not permitted, because it ultimately brings an organization to its knees. The only security that an organization and its people have is in consistently achieving the measurable outcomes that its stakeholders value and expect.
◀ A clear, consistent, frequently updated and relevant vision of where the organization is headed, which is promoted by leaders to reach all staff. This vision must be embraced by most of the members of the organization.
◀ Managers who can inspire both our heads and hearts without unnecessarily discouraging actions.
◀ Managers who are effective delegators and do not micromanage (unless a temporary crisis or problem warrants this approach).
◀ Managers who treat everyone fairly but realize that people are different and respond differently to various approaches to supervision and coaching.
◀ Timely, clear decision-making.
◀ Adequate resources to get the job done.
◀ A positive environment that emphasizes looking for positives rather than only finding fault.
◀ An atmosphere where a sense of humor is valued and encouraged.
◀ Fairness.
◀ Acknowledgement and appropriate reward of achievement.
◀ Managers who want to be liked but work for respect, not popularity.

I recall receiving an encouraging phone call from the Chairperson of the Minnesota Board of Regents after my office made an admissions decision that had become very public and controversial. I was criticized in the media and received abusive and threatening e-mails, letters, and calls from the public. Although I was confident in my decision and greatly appreciated the strong backing from the University's President, it was a professional low point for me. I was so moved during the phone call from the Regent that I could barely speak. Some time later, I again thanked the Regent for his phone call and he told me that he often calls a University coach after a big loss because that is when a person needs support the most. If I have been touched by such genuine acts of kindness, how can I not do the same for others?

106

Case
Study

CASE STUDY 11:
"WHAT MAKES A LEADER?"

LESSONS
FOR HIGHER   "Emotional intelligence is the sine qua non
EDUCATION   of leadership" (Goldman 1998).
MANAGERS

Daniel Goleman has studied and written extensively on emotional intelligence. In his highly influential 1998 *Harvard Business Review* article, "What Makes a Leader?" Goleman observed:

> *Every businessperson knows a story about a highly intelligent, highly skilled executive who was promoted into a leadership position only to fail at the job. And they also know a story about someone with solid—but not extraordinary—intellectual abilities and technical skills who was promoted into a similar position and then soared.*
>
> *Such anecdotes support the widespread belief that identifying individuals with the "right stuff" to be leaders is more art than science. After all, the personal styles of superb leaders vary: some leaders are subdued and analytical; others shout their manifestos from the mountaintops. And just as important, different situations call for different types of leadership…. Most mergers need a sensitive negotiator at the helm, whereas many turnarounds require a more forceful authority*
>
> *I have found, however, that the most effective leaders are alike in one crucial way: they all have a high degree of what has come to be known as emotional intelligence. It's not that IQ and technical skills are irrelevant. They do matter, but mainly as "threshold capabilities;" that is, they are the entry-level requirements for executive positions. But my research, along with other recent studies, clearly shows that emotional intelligence is the sine qua non of leadership. Without it, a person can have the best training in the world, an incisive, analytical mind, and an endless supply of smart ideas, but he still won't make a great leader.*

Goleman also outlines how you can tell if someone has high emotional intelligence and how you can recognize it in yourself. Goleman identifies five components of emotional intelligence:

◖ Self-awareness
◖ Self-regulation
◖ Motivation
◖ Empathy
◖ Social skill

CASE STUDY 12:
"CAN EMOTIONAL INTELLIGENCE BE LEARNED?"

LESSONS FOR HIGHER EDUCATION MANAGERS	A person's genetics impacts their emotional intelligence. However, research and practice clearly demonstrates that emotional intelligence can be learned (Goleman 1998).

In his *Harvard Business Review* article on "What Makes A Leader?" Goleman (1998) includes a side-bar section entitled, "Can Emotional Intelligence Be Learned?" Several excerpts of this section are included here because it is especially helpful in understanding why some leaders are not strong in the emotional intelligence aspects of leadership and management.

> *For ages, people have debated if leaders are born or made. So too goes the debate about emotional intelligence. Are people born with certain levels of empathy, for example, or do they acquire empathy as a result of life's experiences? The answer is both. Scientific inquiry strongly suggests that there is a genetic component to emotional intelligence. Psychological and developmental research indicates that nurture plays a role as well. How much of each perhaps will never be known, but research and practice clearly demonstrate that emotional intelligence can be learned.*
>
> *One thing is certain: emotional intelligence increases with age. There is an old-fashioned word for the phenomenon: maturity. Yet even with maturity, some people still need training to enhance their emotional intelligence. Unfortunately, far too many training programs that intend to build leadership skills—including emotional intelligence—are a*

waste of time and money. The problem is simple: they focus on the wrong part of the brain.

Emotional intelligence is born largely in the neuro-transmitters of the brain's limbic system, which governs feelings, impulses, and drives. Research indicates that the limbic system learns best through motivation, extended practice and feedback. Compare this with the kind of learning that goes on in the neocortex, which governs analytical and technical ability. The neocortex grasps concepts and logic…. Not surprisingly—but mistakenly—it is also the part of the brain targeted by most training programs aimed at enhancing emotional intelligence. When such programs take, in effect, a neocortical approach, my research with the Consortium for Research on Emotional Intelligence in Organizations has shown they can even have a negative impact on people's job performance.

To enhance emotional intelligence, organizations must refocus their training to include the limbic system. They must help people break old behavioral habits and establish new ones. That not only takes much more time than conventional training programs, it also requires an individualized approach.

Case
Study

CASE STUDY 13:
"LEADERSHIP THAT GETS RESULTS"

LESSONS
FOR HIGHER
EDUCATION
MANAGERS

Goleman describes six leadership styles and highlights the combination of styles that promote the very best climate and business performance.

In his March-April 2000 *Harvard Business Review* article, "Leadership That Gets Results," Daniel Goleman outlines research,

…by the Hay/McBer consulting firm, which draws on a random sample of 3,871 executives selected from a database of more than 20,000 executives worldwide. The article takes much of the mystery out of effective leadership. The research found six distinct leadership styles, each springing from different components of emotional intelligence. The styles, taken individually, appear to have a direct and unique impact on the working atmosphere of a company, division, or team, and in turn, on its financial performance.

In his article, Goleman describes each of the six leadership styles.

*Coercive leaders demand immediate compliance. **Authoritative** leaders mobilize people toward a vision. **Affiliative** leaders create emotional bonds and harmony. **Democratic** leaders build consensus through participation. **Pacesetting** leaders expect excellence and self-direction. And **coaching** leaders develop people for the future....*

Many studies, including this one, have shown that the more styles a leader exhibits, the better. Leaders who have mastered four or more—especially the authoritative, democratic, affiliative, and coaching styles—have the very best climate and business performance. And the most effective leaders switch flexibly among the leadership styles as needed....

....
CASE STUDY 14:
WHY DREAM TEAMS FAIL

☀
Case
Study

LESSONS
FOR HIGHER
EDUCATION
MANAGERS

It takes individually talented people to win. But they must blend their various talents into a coherent, working team.

We need to celebrate the contributions of "role" players as much as we do the stars.

In a very illuminating article on "Why Dream Teams Fail," Geoffrey Colvin (2006) observes "If someone tells you you're being recruited onto a dream team, maybe you should run. In our team-obsessed age, the concept of the dream team has become irresistible. But it's brutally clear that they often blow up. Why? Because they're not teams. They're just bunches of people."

Colvin lists the most common paths to failure:

◀ Signing too many all-stars.
◀ Failing to build a culture of trust.
◀ Tolerating competing agendas.
◀ Letting conflicts fester.
◀ Hiding from the real issues.

Colvin wraps up his article with the following observation:

In business, dream teams are usually part of some rescue fantasy, not the real world.... To avoid seducing yourself into thinking all your problems might be vaporized by assembling a dream team, resolve now to accept this fact: There was only one Dream Team, and that was the 1992 U.S. Olympic basketball team. Michael Jordan, Magic Johnson, Larry Bird, Charles Barkley, Patrick Ewing—it was a one-time event. (And remember, Bird and Magic, the veteran co-captains, both had reputations as team players.) For the rest of us, putting together a few talented people who will work honestly and rigorously for something greater than themselves—that's more than enough of a dream.

7

PURPOSE

Outlines the strategies and tactics that will be employed to achieve an organization's mission and goals

OUTCOMES

Ensuring success through effective strategic and tactical planning

Tri-O

OUTCOME
PLANNING TOOLS

*If your plan is not in writing, you
do not have a plan at all...
You may have a dream, a vision, or
perhaps most often — a nightmare.*

~ GERALD A. MICHAELSON (1987)

In white water rafting, you and your team enter the river at a relatively calm spot. Once you begin to hit the rapids, on most rivers, there are also periods of floating over calm water. However, for much of the trip down river, the best you can do is hang on, not fall out of the raft and try to keep the raft from hitting the rocks and capsizing. You do your best to successfully navigate the river until you reach your destination downstream.

Most planning and preparation for the trip should have already been done before you move the raft into the river at the starting point. The hectic and demanding conditions along the way only allow for making adjustments to the original plan.

Effective preparation is vital to staying on course toward successful outcomes in higher education. That's what the Tri-O Outcome

CHAPTER 7 *Tri-O Outcome Planning Tools*

Planning Tools component is about: ensuring success through effective strategic and tactical planning.

Key Questions for Planning

Everett T. Suters (1976) defines *planning* as "...the process of determining where you want to go and how you want to get there." Suters lists a set of questions that are helpful to managers as they go through the planning process:

1. *Where are we now?*
2. *Where will we end up if we follow our present path?*
3. *Where do we want to go?*
4. *What do we have to do to get us where we want to go (the achieving of our objectives) and how does it affect our situation as it exists today?*
5. *When will we achieve our objectives?*
6. *Who is going to carry out the plans?*
7. *What will the implementation of our plans require in the way of financial, production, material and human resources?*
8. *Is the overall plan practical? Can we accomplish it or will we have to modify it?*

The Importance of Planning

Suters (1976) outlines some of the advantages of planning:

1. *Provides positive action. No one plans to fail. People plan to succeed. It promotes a positive attitude.*
2. *Involves the participation of other members of your group.*
3. *Promotes understanding as to what is to be done.*
4. *Promotes good organization and focuses attention on the objectives, counteracting task-oriented activity.*
5. *Promotes good leadership. People know what it is that they want to accomplish.*
6. *Creates an atmosphere of professional-type management in the group.*
7. *Identifies risks and enables you to assess them.*
8. *Leads to action. Planning "makes something happen," with a positive thrust.*

Much of strategic and tactical planning is an intellectual process. Gerald A. Michaelson points out that, "The foundation of strategy is in the mental process, not in some physical act" (Michaelson 1987).

My spouse and I recently moved into a new house built from a custom design that was developed by working with an architect/ builder. This process illustrates the demands of planning as well as the importance of effective planning.

The steps that led to the development of the final design and blueprint for the new house required many hours of thinking about options and talking with the architect to translate ideas to paper. Making changes to the design on paper is relatively inexpensive, but once construction begins it is expensive to make changes.

Effective planning, well in advance, pays off for organizations in very visible and meaningful ways. It saves valuable time, energy, and fiscal resources. It is also a major factor in loading the deck in your favor. Effective planning is absolutely vital for organizational success.

Strategies and Tactics

Tri-O Outcome Planning Tools facilitate the development of effective strategies and tactics that will be employed to achieve an organization's mission and goals.

Strategies are blueprints that outline what an organization needs to do to be successful. A strategy is a plan of action for accomplishing a specific goal.

Tactics are methods used to operationalize the strategy.

If you do not identify the right strategies, the right tactics will not emerge. Tactics are relatively easy to select if the strategies are apt. The challenge with tactics is their effective execution.

Gerald A. Michaelson (1987) makes several important observations about strategies and tactics:

> *It is a marketing fundamental that the strategy must be correct for the organization to succeed. There's no chicken and egg problem here. The strategy must be right first; then the tactics can support the strategy. Excellent strategy at higher levels can sustain many tactical failures at lower levels. The converse is rarely true. Sustained tactical*

116

success—even continuous, brilliant execution of tactics—seldom over-
comes an inadequate strategic posture.

A bad strategy supported by good tactics can even be a fast route to
failure as, for example, driving fast and skillfully in the wrong direc-
tion does not get you to your destination.

In thinking about strategies and tactics, I am reminded of the story
about a person who brought his car to a garage and complained to
the technician that the car kept cutting off. The technician looked
under the hood, thought for a minute, grabbed a hammer and made
a single tap on the motor. The car began to run like a top. The technician gave the car owner a bill for $50. The car owner promptly
objected by saying it only took a minute to hit the motor one time,
which should not cost $50! The technician replied that the car owner
was correct. He took back the bill and rewrote it to say: "The charge
for hitting the motor is $1. The charge for knowing where to hit the
motor is $49."

In this story, the car owner was paying the technician $49 for the
strategy and $1 for the tactic. The moral: The strategy must be cor-
rect or the tactics likely will not work.

Requirements for Developing a Successful Outcome Plan

The Tri-O Outcome Plan outlines the strategies and tactics that will
be employed to achieve an organization's mission and goals. The Tri-
O planning component focuses on producing an action plan that will
be used to guide the work of an organization.

There are three absolute requirements for developing a successful
outcome plan. They must be:

◀ in writing;
◀ relatively simple; and
◀ developed by a "plan-by-doing" approach.

Advantages of A Written Plan

The intellectual process of planning must result in a written document. Writing the plan down requires the discipline to think through
what and how you plan to accomplish something, and then critically

examine your plan. It's also much easier to have a written plan that your staff can refer to instead of trying to improvise.

Simplicity Facilitates Action

Tri-O Outcome Plans are built on the premise that simple is better!

While some higher education leaders fail to take time to produce a written planning document, others put so much information on paper that the document loses its ability to direct the work of an organization. Like a mission statement that is so long that it cannot be memorized easily, a planning document can be too detailed.

If an outcome plan is too complicated or detailed, two things are likely to happen. It will either

◀ confuse those attemting to implement it, or

◀ sit on a shelf and not get used.

It is common to read in the sports pages that a team that has not been successful chooses to "go back to basics" and simplify its game plan. Similarly, many corporations that are conglomerates often periodically choose to shed some of their business units to focus on its "core" businesses. Many businesses will also focus on reducing the number of personnel reporting lines to streamline decision-making.

Jack Welch, former CEO of General Electric and management expert, reinforces the importance of not making strategy too complicated. With a doctorate in Chemical Engineering, Welch is certainly able to grasp complex theories; yet he advocates a straightforward approach to strategy.

> *More than a few times over the past three years, I have been on a speaking program or at a business conference with one big strategy guru or another. And more than a few times, I have listened to their presentations in disbelief.*
>
> *It's not that I don't understand their theories about competitive advantage, core competencies, virtual commerce, supply-chain economics, disruptive innovation, and so on. It's just that the way these experts tend to talk about strategy—as if it is some kind of high-brain scientific methodology—feels really off to me.*

*I know that strategy is a living, breathing, totally dynamic game.
Forget the arduous, intellectualized number crunching and data grind-
ing. In real life, strategy is actually very straightforward. You pick a
general direction and implement like hell.* (Welch and Welch 2005)

The "Plan-by-Doing" Approach

Planning by doing is a corollary of keeping it simple. If we spend so
much time planning that the plan never gets implemented fully, planning has become a process rather than an outcome.

In his book, *Selling the Invisible,* Bob Sevier (2005) highlights Harry
Beckwith's astute observations on the high cost of perfection:

> *Once in a while we all get distracted by the idea of writing a perfect
> plan or making a perfect decision. The fact is, the perfect plan or per-
> fect decision is often too expensive and not worth the cost.*
>
> *…[M]any big-picture thinkers (and companies) are burdened by
> this search for perfection: The perfect plan. The perfect decision. The
> perfect idea. Too often, however, the path to perfection leads through
> procrastination….*
>
> *Don't let perfect ruin good.*

I have benefited greatly in my career by the advice and guidance
that I have received from various mentors. I recall the advice given to
me by John K. Parker, a very successful leader in the nonprofit and
government sectors. While in the process of writing my dissertation
and having expressed concern about how complicated the process
was, John stressed to me that I should "produce, not perfect!"

John reminded me that I could write the book, one of my life's goals,
later, but that my immediate objective was to produce a quality dissertation and earn my doctorate. I have used John Parker's advice repeat-
edly in my professional career whenever I am getting bogged down in
the planning and implementation processes. Produce, don't perfect!

I was also greatly influenced in my approach to management and
planning by Richard Van Horn, the President of the University of
Houston and later the President of the University of Oklahoma. I
worked with Dr. Van Horn during his time at Houston and benefited
greatly from his brilliance as a strategist. He frequently reminded

me to "plan by doing." He meant that you should have goals and the short-term and intermediate steps in mind to achieve them. But once this is done, you must begin implementing your plan. You may need to make frequent adjustments along the way but you must make concrete progress toward achieving your goals rather than being stalled by "paralysis by analysis."

In *Business Week's* cover story "Speed Demons: How smart companies are creating new products—and whole new businesses—almost overnight," Hamm and Rowley (2006a) observe that "[s]peed is emerging as the ultimate competitive weapon." One of the ultimate examples of planning-by-doing is provided in a related article describing a small and agile software firm, 37signals LLC.

> *Back in the old days—say 2003—it typically took a couple of years for a software product to go from bright idea to market. Nowadays? Try months. 37signals LLC, a small Chicago company, has an iron-clad rule: Never take more than 3½ months to get a product out the door, not counting holidays or vacations….*
>
> *In fact, 37signals turns the old ways upside down. For starters, its applications are delivered on the Web for a monthly fee, not sold in boxes. The company's seven employees don't believe in planning either. They just start creating and trying things out. And rather than loading products with bells and whistles, they design them to do a few things well…. 'The way to get really good software is to make the simplest thing you can as fast as you can and get reaction, then see where it goes from there,' says, Paul Graham, a pioneer in Web-based software and now a guru for software entrepreneurs who operate like those at 37signals.* (Hamm and Rowley 2006b)

Customer Service as Strategy

I have said before that higher education remains unwilling to acknowledge that it has customers. I also believe that the consistent, effective application of a customer service model is alien to much of higher education. Effective customer service strengthens the stakeholder-focus and outcome-orientation of the Tri-O system.

While the following observation featured in *Sales and Marketing Management* is directed at the world of business, it has definite implications for higher education as well, especially given the significant increases in tuition and fees in recent years.

> *...On the grandest scale, every point of service delivery is a time when customers evaluate whether they have gotten their money's worth, whether the price they have paid equals or exceeds the value of what they are getting and what they were promised.* (Liswood 1987)

The importance of customer service is reinforced by Davidow and Uttal (1989).

> *Though nobody has developed a general model of service costs and benefits and applied it to different industries, we can confidently make one assertion: In all industries, when competitors are roughly matched, those that stress customer service will win.*

The Strategic Service Vision and the Value Equation

Tri-O is stakeholder-focused and outcome-oriented. Effective customer service should be one of the key strategies of all higher education programs. In developing effective customer service strategies and tactics, I recommend the work of service marketing experts such as James L. Heskett, Leonard L. Berry, A. Parasuraman, and Valarie A. Zeithaml.

In Chapter 5, I discussed the work of James L. Heskett, Professor Emeritus at the Harvard Business School. Heskett developed what he terms the "strategic service vision" that, "...provides a framework for developing a set of shared 'core' values, practices, and measures as part of an overall strategy."

Heskett notes that entrepreneurs implement the strategic service vision by keeping in mind what he and his colleagues call the "value equation."

> *Whether purchasing a product or service, entering into an employment agreement, or making a grant to a not-for-profit organization, people want value. But just what is value? While social entrepreneurs rarely take time to define it, they implicitly understand and endeavor to deliver it. The value equation, based on extensive observation, makes an effort to define it. It can be depicted as:*

$$\text{Value (for clients, staff,}\atop\text{volunteers, donors, etc.)} = \frac{Results + Process\ Quality}{Cost + Ease\ of\ Access}$$

This doesn't, of course, include all the considerations involved in a particular transaction, but it highlights the important ones....
(Heskett 2002)

Heskett notes that "The value equation is based on the simple tenet that people do not buy products or services; they buy results." Heskett indicates that in the value equation, "...*results* are measured in terms of things desired by a 'customer.'" Heskett (1998) further explains that:

Value can be enhanced by increasing either of the elements in the numerator of the equation or cutting either of the elements in the denominator, while holding all other elements constant. But astute managers have found that it is important to make progress on all four fronts simultaneously.

The Value Equation at the New York City Police Department

The value equation is based on the simple tenet that people do not buy products or services; they buy results. This is as true of employees in an organization as it is of the "customers" served by the organization...It describes a set of basic assumptions under which remarkable results were achieved in just three years by the NYPD, during which major crime in the city was cut roughly in half at little additional budgetary cost to its citizens. (Heskett 1998)

Case Study 15, "Producing Results By Proactive Actions And Not Just Reacting" (on page 132), provides an overview of the Compstat system as it was developed by the New York City Police Department and adapted by other police departments throughout the country. Compstat is an excellent example of how managers can proactively influence factors that are seemingly out of their control and achieve very positive results for their stakeholders. Compstat is about playing offense as well as defense.

Service Quality

Marketing experts Berry, Parasuraman, and Zeithaml (1988) provide a look at service quality that is very helpful when managers are developing strategy for their organization. The following are excerpts from their *Business Horizons* article, "The Service-Quality Puzzle."

> *Quality is conformance to customer specifications; it is the customer's definition of quality, not management's, that counts.*
>
> *Customers assess service quality by comparing what they want or expect to what they actually get or perceive they are getting. To earn a reputation for quality, an organization must meet—or exceed—customer expectations.*
>
> *And what do service customers expect? Our research suggests these expectations cover five areas:*
> * *Tangibles: the physical facilities, equipment, appearance of personnel;*
> * *Reliability: the ability to perform the desired service dependably, accurately, and consistently;*
> * *Responsiveness: the willigness to provide prompt service and help customers;*
> * *Assurance: employees' knowledge, courtesy, and ability to convey trust and confidence; and*
> * *Empathy: the provision of caring, individualized attention to customers.*

Strategies and Tactics in Action

An example of a major *strategy* in the Office of Admissions at the University of Minnesota–Twin Cities is our commitment to providing "extra mile" customer service. This strategy has been the foundation for the work of our entire office for over 14 years. We strongly believe that by serving others, we also serve ourselves. While we sometimes fall short of our goal of "extra mile" customer service, we are deeply committed to this strategy and it guides almost all of our major operational, budget, and staffing decisions. It is now ingrained into our culture. We believe that customer service provides the university with a significant competitive advantage in our efforts to recruit and enroll an outstanding undergraduate class.

With a fall 2006 enrollment of over 50,000 students, the Twin Cities Campus is one of the largest college campuses in the United States. A large campus can provide students with many opportunities. It can also cause students to fear that they will be treated as a number instead of an individual. Our campus has devoted considerable time, energy, and money, especially throughout the last fifteen years, to improve the undergraduate experience for students. This effort is paying off in dramatic improvements in student satisfaction surveys and in student retention and timely graduation. The improved "word of mouth advertising" has also contributed to dramatic increases in the number of applications for admission that the university receives each year.

An example of a *tactic* designed to operationalize our "extra mile" customer service strategy can be found in our Office of Admissions Call Center. We face the same challenges of finite funding that almost all programs in higher education face. We know that we can save money by implementing a computer-supported telephone "call tree" to initially handle the calls to our main office telephone number. However, we consciously choose to staff our Call Center with student assistants so that calls are received by a person instead of a computer. We also staff the Call Center with a sufficient number of students so that the wait time does not irritate callers. A key outcome was that on December 15, 2005, the day of the fall freshman priority application deadline, our average hold time was only 14 seconds.

The realities of a very large campus and our office's strong commitment to effectively serving our students, led to the staffing of our Admissions Call Center with student assistants. We find that our callers are pleasantly surprised to talk with a person when they call instead of a computer-supported message. Our student assistants are selected and trained to be friendly and helpful. Because of this, we are able to respond to our callers' needs in a more effective manner. We are also able to refer them, when necessary, to other personnel in our office or at the University.

We choose to invest very precious fiscal and human resources in our Call Center because we have learned the important distinction between being efficient and being effective. Chapter 4 emphasized that one of the six basic assumptions of the Tri-O system is an under-standing of the difference between being efficient and being effective (*see* page 54).

Being effective does not mean that efficiency should suffer. It means, however, that taking an action that helps us achieve our outcomes is more critical than having a process that primarily focuses on saving money. The benefits we derive from staffing our Call Center with stu-dent assistants means that we choose to be effective somewhat at the price of being efficient. Since operating funds have limits, we work hard to save costs by realizing operating efficiencies in other aspects of our office operation. This represents a key strategic and tactical deci-sion of our office. But we respect that other programs might make a different decision based on their own strategic and tactical planning.

Tri-O Planning Tools

Written Outcome Plans

In the Office of Admissions at Minnesota, we sometimes find it appropriate to develop very detailed written outcome plans. This is especially the case when we present our outcome plans to anyone outside our office, namely stakeholders. On these occasions, we take great care to make certain that both the content and appearance of the plans garner the confidence of the stakeholders. We seek to ensure that these action plans are as sophisticated and effective as any that would be produced by a top national management consulting firm. The packaging and appearance of outcome plans for high-stakes projects is integral to their successful adoption by stakeholders.

Tri-O Diagram Format

For the vast majority of our outcome plans, simplicity and a plan-by-doing approach are emphasized. Therefore, our outcome plans often take the form of a diagram or a chart. Building visual diagrams or models often helps clarify a complex process. Diagrams illustrate the problem or project at hand without reams of written pages.

Strategic Level Outcome Plan

In the Minnesota Office of Admissions, we often try to reduce our strategic outcome plans to a single diagram. Figure 7.1, "The Road to Successful Enrollment" (on page 126), provides an example of the major strategic stages that we go through in enrolling a freshman class. It does not detail the tactical steps to take for a successful recruitment cycle, but outlines the strategies from a "macro" viewpoint. This overview approach highlights the big picture so we don't get lost in the details of the outcome plan.

While the diagram consists of just one page, it is based on my office's review of the literature, research and experience, and years of professional judgment. The planning that goes into the development of the diagram is detailed and sophisticated, but the diagram is reduced to the simplest form possible so that it is an easily understood snapshot and a guide to our work.

Tactical Level Outcome Plan

Table 7.1 (on page 127) summarizes one aspect of an outcome plan for recruiting the freshman class at Minnesota and outlines tactics used at each major strategic stage of the recruitment cycle.

The "funnel" column refers to the well-known "admissions funnel" concept. Essentially, a prospective student moves (or does not move) through various stages of interest in an institution. Each stage in the "admissions funnel" is critical because we want to encourage each prospective student to move through the next stage until (assuming it is a good fit for the student and the University) they enroll at our institution.

The Admissions staff in the Minnesota Office of Admissions has divided the "admissions funnel" into four primary recruitment stages:
- Project Filling the basket
- Project Choice Set
- Project Application
- Project Commitment

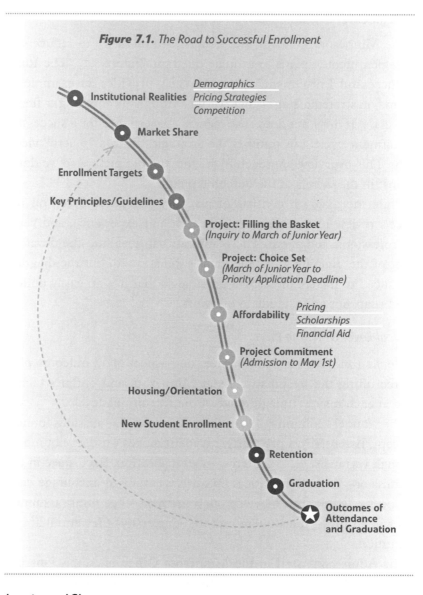

Figure 7.1. The Road to Successful Enrollment

Laminated Sheets

The technique of using laminated sheets was borrowed from football coaches. During games, football coaches frequently refer to one or two pieces of paper that have been laminated in plastic.

Coaches spend hours developing game plans for each game based on the competition and other factors. The team's major offensive and defensive schemes (strategies) and plays (tactics) are usually con-

Table 7.1: *Sample Freshman Recruitment Plan
(Goals of Freshman Admissions Program, University of Minnesota)*

FUNNEL	STRATEGIES	TACTICS (LEADS TO ACHIEVEMENT OF GOALS)
Hit University of Minnesota Freshman Enrollment Targets		
Filling the Basket	Increase number of inquirers	◀ Purchase very targeted mailing lists
Project Choice Set	Encourage campus visits, get updated student info., grade interest	◀ Targeted e-mail invitations ◀ Employ predictive modeling screen
Project Application	Get applications and enhance customer service	◀ Targeted telecounseling
Project Commitment	Meet confirmation targets	◀ Appropriate number of admits by college ◀ Targeted e-mail and telecounseling reception invitations

tained in a thick binder of papers called a playbook. The playbook is carefully monitored to ensure that it does not fall into the hands of a competitor.

Since the coaches cannot refer to a bulky playbook during the game, they summarize their game plan for that particular game on several sheets of paper. The game plan is a summary of the major offensive and defensive strategies and tactics to be used for that game, based on an assessment of the strengths and weakness of their own team and reviews of game films of their opponent. The laminated sheets may contain many items, but often they include the various plays (tactics) that will be used in specific game situations, (*e.g.*, third down and long yardage). Teams laminate the game plans in plastic to make them more durable and to protect them from the weather.

At Minnesota, we summarize detailed outcome plans into one or two pages so that we can frequently refer to them and reinforce them with staff. The format of the one- or two-page laminated sheet (as outlined in Figure 7.1, on page 126) is a very helpful way to make certain that we keep our action plans sufficiently simple. We laminate the sheets not for protection from the weather, but to make them durable for the frequent use they get during the recruitment cycle.

128

Figure 7.2. *Transfer Admissions Dream House*
University of Minnesota–Twin Cities

	APPLICATION PROCESSING & REVIEW	COMMUNICATIONS	RECRUITMENT/ TRANSFER SERVICES
Third Floor 2008		◀ Prospective student communications cycle ◀ Customized viewbook, transfer edition ◀ Transfer blog	◀ Enhanced visit program publicity ◀ MnCAP[1]–expand Community College options ◀ Enhance MnCAP[1] communications
Second Floor 2007		◀ Develop virtual tours for transfers ◀ Enhanced transfer applicant communications cycle	◀ Expanded on-campus housing for transfers ◀ Early transfer orientation ◀ Transfer Ambassadors ◀ Enhance student of color recruitment plan
First Floor 2006			Transfer–Living Learning housing community ✓
Ground Floor 2005	Transfer application processing reengineering ✓	Transfer applicant communications cycle ✓	◀ Transfer and International Admissions Welcome Center ✓ ◀ MnCAP[1] Web site ✓ ◀ Student of color recruitment plan ✓
Current Services	◀ Transfer application processing and review ◀ Scholarship application processing and review	◀ Transfer Student Guide & application ◀ Online application for admission[4] ◀ Online status check	◀ Comprehensive visit program ◀ Online visit reservations ◀ MnCAP[1]

[1] Minnesota Cooperative Admissions Program (guaranteed admission program with area community colleges)
[2] DARwin: Degree Audit Reporting System (licensed from Miami University of Ohio)
[3] Course Applicability System (licensed from Miami University of Ohio) in cooperation with the Minnesota State College and University system.

The "Dream House" Diagnostic/Planning Approach

A very useful approach to identifying effective strategies and tactics is to develop a blueprint for a program's "dream house." A "dream house" approach encourages thinking about the most important elements of a program's success and requires the fundamental parts to be built first. Each floor is then added in order of importance. Future floors can be diagrammed in the blueprint to show where the pro-

ADVISING	TRANSFER ARTICULATION	TECHNOLOGY TOOLS	
	Curriculum meetings– Community Colleges and UMTC depts.	Online advising services, 24/7	**Third Floor 2008**
◀ Community College Counselor Advisory committee ◀ Transfer Student Advisory committee ◀ Business-related major information session	Articulated (2+2) programs listed centrally	◀ KSIs for TCE, LE, and CLA staff workload[7] ◀ Electronic transcripts ◀ Transfer recruitment database	**Second Floor 2007**
Health science information session ✓		◀ CAS[3] widely available ✓ ◀ Transfer credit evaluation KSIs[7] ✓	**First Floor 2006**
CLA, CFANS, CBS[6] information sessions ✓		◀ Re-engineer transfer credit processing ✓ ◀ Online knowledge base & e-mail handling[5] ✓ ◀ Application processing dashboards ✓	**Ground Floor 2005**
◀ Prospective transfer student college specific advising sessions ◀ Individual advising appointments	Transfer guides	Transfer credit evaluations utilizing DARwin[2]	**Current Services**

[4] Created and hosted by Royall & Company.
[5] Licensed from RightNow Technologies.
[6] College of Liberal Arts, College of Food, Agricultural and Natural Resource Sciences, College of Biological Sciences
[7] Key Success Indicators, Transfer Credit Evaluation, Liberal Education, College of Liberal Arts
✓ Achieved

gram is headed since the "dream house" can, and must, be changed through experience.

The Tri-O "Dream House" Diagnostic/Planning approach has several benefits for higher education managers. A "dream house" diagram is:

◀ Easier to produce. It requires significantly fewer words than a written document.

◀ Much easier to update than a detailed written document.
◀ Much easier to understand than a detailed written document. This is a special advantage for persons outside the program that may not have thorough knowledge about the subject and do not have the time or inclination to plow through details.

Just as with designing and building a real dream house to live in, the planning process requires a diagnosis of where we are right now. My advice in designing a dream house, for either a new program or refining one already in place, is to not obsess about what you don't have. Instead:

◀ Identify the key elements/services that are currently in place. Put these items in the "current" service level of the dream house.
◀ Identify the highest priority items to be put in place to make your program successful. Add these to the ground floor.
◀ Add to the future floors of your Tri-O dream house the additional items that will contribute to your program's continued success.
◀ Mark each item as it is completed to illustrate progress.
◀ Keep in mind the concept of "Kaizen." Kaizen is the highly successful approach used by Japanese manufacturers such as Toyota. Toyota continually makes improvements, often in small steps, in its products. It's better to plan by doing and work toward developing a state-of-the art program than it is to be frozen by the despair about what you don't currently practice or have.

Transfer Admissions Dream House

Figure 7.2 (on page 128–129) illustrates our "dream house" for enhancing the undergraduate transfer admissions programs at Minnesota over the course of several years. The basic elements of a very successful transfer program are in place and operating well at Minnesota. However, our office plans to provide more customized services for these important cohorts of prospects that will include an appropriate mix of "high-touch" and "high-tech," or self-help, options to be made available in both one-stop electronic and physical centers.

The Minnesota Center for Transfer and International Admissions was recently established in the Office of Admissions. The intent is to make the center a national prototype for providing effective service to transfer and international students.

The Tri-O Operations Calendar

One of the most discouraging activities in managing a program is constantly reinventing the wheel. Why constantly redo things that were previously produced in our organization? What a waste of precious time and energy!

Figure 7.3. *Sample Office of Admissions Operations Calendar*

Objectives: (1) Keep everyone informed regarding upcoming events, mailings, deadlines, etc.; and (2) look ahead so we are proactive and on track with future projects.

JUNE

Mailings/Publications

Application content deadline	Person A	6/1
Missing prep requirements letter	Person B	6/1
Missing final college transcript letter to admitted transfers	Person B	6/16
Web Site update reminder	All	

Events/Activities/Misc.

Prospective Student Advisory Committee meeting	Person C	6/8
SAT scores from 5/6 test in PeopleSoft	Person D	6/23
Start event Key Service Indicators	Person E	6/26

Deadlines/FYI

SAT test date		6/3
Freshman & parent orientation begins		6/7

JULY

Mailings/Publications

Web Site update reminder	All	
Start sending app acknowledgement	Person H	7/24
Scholarship award notification date	Person G	Late July

Events/Activities/Misc.

Determine status of freshman admission for spring	Person B	7/3
Spring AP info in PeopleSoft	Person D	7/7
College of Biological Sciences prospect event	Person J	7/7
ACT test scores from 6/10 test date in PeopleSoft	Person D	7/14

Deadlines/FYI

University holiday	All	7/4
Spring IB scores available	Person J	7/10
Transfer scholarship application priority deadline	Person M	7/15
Housing assignments mailed	Housing	7/31

132

Most organizations or programs have a natural cycle in which similar activities or events take place each year. The old adage that, "The thinnest paper is stronger than the strongest memory," is relevant here. The Tri-O Operations Calendar is a valuable tool for not wasting time and energy by doing planning already done for the same, or a similar, prior event or project.

In the Minnesota Admissions Program, key actions that must be taken at the same time each year have been identified. This is our Operations Calendar. We go over the actions needed for the current month and upcoming several months with our management team at least once a month to remind them of pending key actions in their area. Items are deleted or added as needed.

We also encourage each unit in the Office of Admissions to build its own Operations Calendar.

Figure 7.3, on page 131, provides an example from the Minnesota Office of Admissions Operations Calendar.

Summary

Strategic and tactical planning can be one of the most mentally taxing and time consuming phases of running an organization. However, neglecting the planning component may lead to failure.

Tri-O is not about losing; it's about winning! The Tri-O Outcome Planning Tools component is about ensuring success though effective strategic and tactical planning.

CASE STUDY 15:
PRODUCING RESULTS BY PROACTIVE ACTIONS
AND NOT JUST REACTING

LESSONS
FOR HIGHER
EDUCATION
MANAGERS

Playing offense instead of defense leads to better outcomes.

Effective leadership and the use of metrics
can help transform an organization.

Compstat began in New York in 1994, under Commissioner [William] Bratton, and the department has credited it as a major factor in the city's precipitous drop in crime. The system maps crime according to precise location and time, providing daily statistics that allow for strategic planning. At the meetings commanders are grilled by their bosses, in front of their peers, about crime trends in their precincts and what is being done about them....(Dewan 2004)

I have been following the media reports on Compstat[5] for years and it has greatly influenced my thinking about the use of data to impact complex issues in a proactive, ongoing fashion and to instill accountability by playing offense instead of defense. Our version of a Compstat approach in the Minnesota Office of Admissions is to track major projects. Compstat has a lot to offer managers in higher education.

However, I am not comfortable with the confrontational aspects of Compstat and have adapted Compstat to be more focused on achieving success rather than confrontations.

The following are excerpts of Shaila Dewan's (2004) article concerning how Compstat use is spreading to police departments around the U.S.:

In the mid-1990s, a new management program called Compstat shook up the New York Police Department. Detectives stopped working 9–5 and started working at the hours most crimes occur. Crime statistics, once compiled every few months, were updated and mapped weekly. Commanders who displayed a feeble grasp of their precinct's problems were summarily replaced. Crime rates raced downward, outpacing a national decline.

Since then, the gospel of New York-style policing—specialized units, statistics-driven deployment, and a startling degree of hands-on leadership—has been spreading throughout the country. So have the people who personify those tactics, a diaspora of zealous former New York Police Department officers who have gone on to lead other departments....

"It's culture shock," said Capt Jeff Fluck, who has been an officer for 27 years in Raleigh, N.C., where a former New York deputy chief, Jane Perlov, now runs the police department. Captain Fluck's job has changed from one that could be left at the office to one in which the phone rings day and night. "It is a paradigm shift like I've never

---

[5] For an excellent description of the Compstat System, see Heskett (1998, 1999, and 2002).

experienced before," he said, adding that the change was long overdue. "It's the difference between responsibility and ownership."

The culture shock goes both ways—the New York chiefs have marveled at commanders who did not commit homicide stats to memory and departments that needed to be persuaded that the police could anticipate and prevent crime. "Basically, they put out fires and kept the lid on things while they were here, and then they went home," Chief Perlov said....

Even without the New York Police Department's ambassadors, Compstat's principles have been rapidly adopted across the country. "Right now, there are so many variations on a theme," said John Firman, the director of research at the International Association of Chiefs of Police. "It's not the New York model anymore. It may be the New Orleans model that went to Baton Rouge."

But the New Yorkers jealously guard Compstat's purity. "They design Compstat meetings and it's nothing more than a staff meeting." Chief Cordero (a former inspector in New York who is now the chief in Newton, Massachusetts) said dismissively. "The accountability isn't there."

But what New York calls accountability, the rest of America may be inclined to call public humiliation. "It's not like it's supposed to be demeaning," said Daniel Fickus, president of the police union in Baltimore, who said the meetings seemed to stifle new ideas. "It's not like you're in school."

Several chiefs said they had toned down the confrontational aspect, shifting the emphasis to sharing information. Peter J. Abbott, chief of police in Sarasota, Fla. who formerly ran a precinct in Queens, calls his version a "kinder, gentler Compstat." Chief Daniel J. Oates, now in Ann Arbor, Mich., calls his "Compstat Ultralite."

8

PURPOSE

Ensures good
stewardship of an
organization's time
and energy and the
accountability for success

OUTCOMES

Reinforces that each
person and each unit in
an organization must
contribute specific
measurable outcomes
that ultimately contribute
to the overall success
of the program

Provides a mechanism
to hold people
accountable for success

Tri-O
DELEGATION
COMPONENT

When you try to run the whole thing yourself, you are forced to make many more quick...judgments. It's like giving a guy a wooden yardstick and asking him to...measure the wavelength of light. He can be Einstein and still have a hard time.

~ JOHN MARSHALL, DESIGN COORDINATOR OF STARS AND
STRIPES '87, THE UNITED STATES' REPRESENTATIVE IN THE 1987
AMERICA'S CUP OCEANGOING YACHT RACE

In any organization outcomes are produced only if the work gets done. Higher education managers can complete some projects single-handedly. But most significant projects require the participation of more than one person, and usually many others. Many projects require a range of skills, experience, and energy not found in only one or two people. Therefore, most higher education managers must enlist others to help with the workload, bring their unique skills and experience to the project, and enable the manager to leverage his or her time. In other words, to survive and excel in their job, managers must delegate effectively.

As with most management functions and tasks, many books and articles are written on the subject of delegation. Despite the wealth of information about delegation, I have found that many higher education managers are not effective delegators. Perhaps they do not think through what it means to delegate effectively. Others move from system to system trying to find the ideal way to delegate.

Sometimes the problem is identifying staff with the appropriate skills and experience to which a task can be delegated. Talented and committed people are an organization's most precious resource; without them, nothing happens in an organization. Their time and energy are scarce commodities, and managers must learn to be effective stewards of this valuable resource.

Stephen Covey (2004), former management professor and enormously successful author and speaker, makes a compelling case for the importance of an organization's people to its success:

> *Twenty or 30 years ago, only 30% of the value added to goods and services came from knowledge work. Now it's 80%. So if companies hope to survive, they must empower people to think for themselves and draw on their experience and wisdom.*

Complicating the delegation function is the reality that many projects require the participation of people in other units or even different organizations that do not report directly to the project manager. The term "delegation" in this book recognizes this reality and assumes that a manager will develop effective relationships with all of the project's participants-a process that is often complex and demanding.

The Tri-O delegation component helps ensure the effective stewardship of the staff's precious time and energy and the accountability for success.

Chapter 2 discusses that the Tri-O Management Operating System is designed to achieve outcomes with a minimum of administrative costs. That's certainly the case with the Tri-O Delegation Component. I have worked through trial and error to develop a component that is both effective and efficient.

Key Elements of the Tri-O Delegation Component
An effective and efficient system of delegation requires:
- ◀ Each person in an organization to produce specific, measurable outcomes;

- Clear agreement on the outcomes to be achieved;
- Accountability;
- Follow-up;
- Each person's unique contribution to be respected and valued; and
- Execution.

Specific, Measurable Outcomes

Most projects in a college or university will involve more than one person. Once two or more people are involved in a project, it is imperative that each project member carry his or her own share of the load and contribute to the achievement of outcomes.

In the Minnesota Admissions Office, we often talk about each staff member owning their own restaurant. We use this metaphor because it's generally the case in any consistently successful restaurant that the owner or her/his general managers must be very actively involved in the business to make certain that the large and small details are handled exceptionally. The glassware and tablecloths must always be absolutely spotless. The service and the food must always be stellar.

The metaphor of owning a restaurant is directly applicable to higher education programs. To be consistently successful, every staff member in the Office of Admissions must "own their own restaurant" every day. This means that each staff member must be clear regarding the outcomes he or she is expected to produce. They are expected to coordinate the resources under their control to produce the expected outcomes.

In our office, we expect our "restaurant owners" to look for and implement best practices in their area. We also expect our managers to be proactive students of their business.

One of my professional joys as a manager is when I am able to say, "I didn't know that we were doing that!" On these occasions, I learn about an aspect of our office that has been improved primarily by the manager and staff of a sub-unit without waiting for "permission" from me or our office's senior management team. The improvements might range from developing a new series of postcards that appeal to prospective students to developing a significantly improved Web site for high school counselors. Obviously, the caveat must be that the staff member developing the new initiative 1) stays within his or her allotted budget and 2) does so to promote the mission of the office. It's great to see a unit flourish because the staff member is excited about his or her work and really owns their own restaurant.

Clear Agreement about Outcomes

In order for each person in an organization to produce specific, measurable outcomes, there must be a clear understanding as to what the individual is expected to produce.

Once there is a clear understanding about outcomes, the project leader should then leave the methods for achieving the outcomes up to the staff member, depending on his or her level of experience, skill, and commitment. Be clear on what needs to be achieved but, to the extent feasible, leave it up to the staff member to determine how the outcomes will be achieved.

Accountability

Unless one person is accountable, no one is accountable.

The foundation of the Tri-O delegation system is that one person, the project manager, makes certain that the project components are on track and result in success.

Follow-up

If it isn't tracked, it doesn't happen.

Projects are generally not successful unless the project manager follows up to make certain that each team member is on track to deliver his or her expected outcomes.

The Tri-O system assumes that everyone wants to do a great job. We must, however, recognize that most people are very busy dealing with multiple tasks and priorities. Even the very best performers can lose sight of key deadlines or get sidetracked by another important task. For this reason, the project manager who wants to be successful simply must have an effective follow-up system in place.

Developing an appropriate follow-up process requires both tact and tenacity. Sometimes follow-up is viewed as not trusting people or not treating them as professionals. This is not the intent of the Tri-O delegation component. It is not disrespectful to recognize that busy people sometimes need reminders. In other words, trust but verify.

Respect and Value Individuals

The Tri-O system values teamwork. An effective team blends the unique skills and contributions of each of its members to create a great outcome. Every project must have a leader. However, the leader will be most effective if they view members of the team as partners, not as people working for them.

How Do Leaders Create Followers?

It's obvious that if a leader wants to delegate responsibilities and duties to others that they must have others willing to assume these duties. In other words, a leader must have followers!

Robert Goffee and Gareth Jones (2001) point out that the sociological and psychological literature on the follower's experience "…tells us that people seek, admire, and respect—that is they follow—leaders who produce within them three emotional responses…"

> *The first is a feeling of **significance**. Followers will give their hearts and souls to authority figures who say, "You really matter," no matter how small the followers' contributions may be….*
>
> *The second emotional resonse followers want from their leaders is a feeling of **community**. Now, there's a messy concept—community. The library is filled with books trying to define it. But for our purposes, let's say community occurs when people feel a unity of purpose around work and, simultaneously, a willingness to relate to one another as human beings….*
>
> *Finally, followers will tell you that a leader is near by when they get a buzzing feeling. People want excitement, challenge, and edge in their lives. It makes them feel engaged in the world. And so, despite all the literature that tells you a leader needn't be **charismatic**, followers will sooner feel leadership from someone who is extroverted and energetic than from someone who isn't. Right or wrong, that's how followers feel.*

Execution

Dick Enberg (2005), CBS golf broadcaster, made the follwing remark during the telecast of a PGA golf tour event after a golfer had failed to make a putt: "Despite lofty position, execute or taste humility." Enberg was relating that, even if you are one of golf's greatest talents, if you don't execute correctly during the round of golf, you will be humbled by defeat.

The best plans in the world will not add value to an organization unless they are carried out with great skill and care. Execution of outcome plans can sometimes be viewed as routine work, but the operations phase is "where the rubber meets the road."

Jamie Dimon, the CEO of JPMorgan Chase, one of the world's biggest financial conglomerates "... pays attention to details." Greg Farrell notes that "...Dimon is reigning in what the visionary has done.... Analysts who follow the company say Dimon is the right man to improve order and efficiency in the array of banks put together by [James] Harrison [former CEO]."

"Sometimes, all that matters are the details," says Dimon...." Sometimes, details will sink you. CEOs should drill down...Strategy and vision are necessary.... But it doesn't work if other things don't work. Execution is the only thing right now. Running the business well and making them shine. That will create its own destiny." (Farrell 2005)

A major part of effective execution is paying attention to the details. The seemingly small details add up to a major impact. The careful and consistent attention to details separates the highly professional operation from one that is amateurish.

The Tri-O Delegation Tracking System

To make the delegation process effective, a manager must have a routine or system in place for appropriate follow-up. The system must have order and predictability. The Tri-O Delegation tracking system fulfills these requirements through two steps:

◀ Projects are divided into various components and a project manager is assigned to each component.

◀ Project sheets are developed with clearly defined milestones and deadlines included.

The complexity of the project and staff resources should determine which tracking system is used. Whatever system is used, remember that Tri-O is designed to be implemented with a minimum amount of staff time and resources. Tri-O will enable you to manage your projects without spending an inordinate amount of time maintaining your tracking system. Keep the system as simple as possible.

There are many project-tracking systems available—some of which utilize computer software. For most projects, however, a relatively simple computer-based spreadsheet is sufficient. Whatever system is used, it must be simple enough to be regularly maintained and monitored by the project manager.

The tracking system can be:

◀ Notes in a notebook

◀ A paper form

◀ A relatively simple computer-based spreadsheet

◀ A computer-based system

In the Minnesota Office of Admissions we use very sophisticated computer software for high stakes, highly complex projects, such as information system upgrades. Such programs define critical paths in a Gannt chart format.

Generally, however, we use a spreadsheet program such as Excel. The advantages of this approach are as follows:

◀ Spreadsheets are easy to maintain and update.

◀ Most staff members are familiar with the rudiments of Excel software.

◀ Training for Excel is readily available.

◀ Distributing sheets electronically can save time and resources.

We find it preferable to update the project sheets after each project meeting and distribute the revised copy before the next project meeting to encourage people to prepare for the meeting.

Table 8.1 is an example of an Excel-based project sheet used, in this case, by our Freshman Outreach Unit. This is the basic format for tracking projects in the Office of Admissions. All managers in our office are familiar with the format.

Table 8.1. *Sample Freshman Recruitment Project Sheet*
(Hit the Numbers by "Extra Mile" Customer Service)

PROJECT	LEADER	DUE DATE	COMMENTS
Red Zone			
Refine group information session script for summer visits	Sue	6/1/03	Revised from 5/1/03
Priority One			
Revise freshman application for fall 2004	David	7/1/03	
Priority Two			
Finalize fall travel schedule	Melissa	9/1/03	Revised from 10/1/03
Priority Three			
Update recruitment activity codes	Catherine	9/1/03	

Don't be misled by the deceptive simplicity of the project sheet approach! Its beauty is its simplicity. Its power is derived from having the organizational discipline to use it.

Project Classification Levels

Each project is classified into one of four priority levels based primarily on its urgency level:

- *Red Zone* projects are given the highest priority either because they have an immediate due date or are behind schedule. We try to include only a very few projects in this category.
- *Priority One* projects are the next highest priority. They are usually the projects that are "on deck" to be moved into the *Red Zone*.
- *Priority Two* projects are usually the projects that are important but not the most urgent.
- *Priority Three* and *Priority Four* projects. We rarely get around to discussing these projects. However, we find it helpful to keep

projects listed in these categories to aid our "corporate memory" and for future planning.

Project Meetings

Project meetings are conducted routinely by the project manager to
track the successful completion of each component of the project.

Face-to-face meetings that are focused and kept short are generally the most effective and respectful way to check in on the progress
of project components. Reports distributed by computer have their
place, but the Tri-O system recognizes that people are an organization's most precious resource. The system must also facilitate the
development of trust and teamwork. There is no substitute for per-
son-to-person discussions to foster a clear understanding of project
status and to promote a team work climate.

Remember—If the project tracking system is not simple and too
time consuming, it will not be used! A system is worthless if it goes
unused. The Tri-O Project Tracking System is relatively simple, not
overly time consuming, and it works!

Growing Leaders

In trying to develop future leaders for our office, I find that staff,
especially those who are relatively inexperienced, are sometimes
reluctant to take on a challenging project. Indeed, staff may feel they
are being punished when assigned an especially difficult project.

It sometimes takes a lot of time and patience with some staff before
they are willing or able to step up and volunteer for a challenging
project. Sometimes it's a lack of experience, but they also often need
encouragement to gain the confidence to try their wings. It is one of
the most rewarding parts of my work to see managers grow into the
level of skill and confidence where they are not only effective leaders
but also mentors to others in the office.

Opportunity often comes wrapped in problems. Some of the best
opportunities for personal growth and advancement have come when
I have taken on an assignment that has the potential for significant success but demanded that major challenges and problems be tackled.

I recall the great advice given by Henry Rossi, former Dean of Admissions at St. John's University in New York City. Henry made this astute observation during a speech he delivered while President of the American Association of Collegiate Registrars and Admissions Officers: "You will never get the gravy if you pass the hot potato."

We all need to remember that "hot potatoes" are often valuable opportunities.

A Final Reminder on Delegation

The Tri-O Delegation component will help you become a more effective manager. At the same time, managers must remember that they can delegate authority but not responsibility. Just as managers expect staff to own their own restaurants, they must do the same!

☼
Case
Study

CASE STUDY 16:
ACCOUNTABILITY

LESSONS
FOR HIGHER
EDUCATION
MANAGERS

Unless there is accountability, not much gets accomplished.

Ultimately, the persons responsible for managing the process must be accountable for outcomes.

David Chanen's 2005 *Minneapolis Star Tribune* article provides an illustration from the law enforcement community highlighting the importance of accountability. Following are excerpts from the article of special relevance:

> *[Minneapolis police department leaders] …decided a specific and intensive two-month strategy was needed to attack gang violence. With the guidance of a national law enforcement expert known as "Junkyard Dog," (Chuck Wexler), the return of a gang expert who had been assigned outside the department and collaboration with other criminal justice system partners, the Minneapolis Strategic Safety Partnership was hatched.*

> *Capt. Mike Martin was asked to return to the department from his leadership role at the state Gang Strike Force to run the intensive gang initiative for July and August. And he had to get the job done with **limited resources.***

*Martin took command of narcotics, organized crime, community response teams and the new Strategic Tactical Operations (STOP) unit that was designed to respond quickly to high-crime areas. Everybody involved received a daily intelligence update on gang and other crime activities. He assigned **clear ownership** and **accountability** for specific gang and problem areas and leveraged resources from other agencies....*

Martin also wanted to reduce duplicative investigative efforts. Take the case of the Tre Tre Crips gang and a Richfield gun shop robbery involving some of its members. Richfield police, the ATF, the state Gang Strike Force and at least five units of the Minneapolis Police Department each had a particular piece of the case, but nobody was in charge and information wasn't being effectively exchanged, he said. So all intelligence was directed through a Minneapolis sergeant.

The effort appears to have reduced homicides, with only eight during July and August. That's down from 12 during the same period last year. In addition, only one of the 13 homicides since July 1 was gang-related.

While Martin said the strategy definitely was the reason for the reduction in homicides, he and other department officials admit they now have to work on bringing down the number of aggravated assaults, robberies and burglaries. There have been nearly 1,500 more of these crimes this year compared with the same period last year.

[Chief of Police] McManus said he wishes the strategy and its resources could have gone beyond two months, but that the department will retain the "best practices" while trying to fix problems such as a rise in domestic aggravated assaults, overlap in drug enforcement and a more effective way to deal with the high number of weapons cases.

9

PURPOSE

Ensures good stewardship of an organization's fiscal and physical resources

OUTCOMES

Ensures that an organization's fiscal and physical resources are effectively devoted to achieving its goals

Tri-O Budget

STEWARDSHIP
COMPONENT

*What your organization gets in the future
depends on what you do with what you have
today. That's what stewardship is all about.*

~ WAYNE SIGLER

The primary goal of this chapter is to stress that resources and influence will go to the organizations whose managers *actively demonstrate* that they are achieving the measurable outcomes that their stakeholders value and expect. That's why this chapter is much more about good stewardship than it is about the mechanics of the budget process. Nonetheless, the mechanics of the budget process are important and will be addressed.

The Tri-O Delegation Component, described in Chapter 8 (on page 135), deals with the stewardship of people's time and energy. The Tri-O Budget Stewardship Component ensures that fiscal (budget) and physical (equipment and office space) resources are devoted to achieving the organization's goals and are used wisely.

CHAPTER 9 *Tri-O Budget Stewardship Component*

152

Key Budget Realities

Budgets are often viewed as complex and boring by many staff members. Staff know that money, equipment, and space are very important, but they often view the process of securing these resources, and especially accounting for them, as someone else's responsibility.

In order for all staff in an organization to fully appreciate the importance of good stewardship of fiscal and physical resources, three key budget realities must be understood and periodically reinforced:

◀ *Resources are finite; there are definite limits.* In any organization, especially large ones, there is always a tendency to feel that the organization has plenty of resources that are simply difficult to access. Managers of a program or unit must educate themselves and their staff on how the larger organization secures and uses its resources so that the resources devoted to their unit are placed in a larger, realistic context. There is no magic checkbook to produce unlimited fiscal resources.

◀ *We must all make difficult budget decisions.* If we don't make the difficult decisions for our own programs, someone else will do it for us.

◀ *An organization's fiscal and physical resources are a means to an end; not an end unto themselves.* While resources are critical, they are only a tool to accomplish the organization's objectives. Everyone must be accountable to use the resources under their control to produce expected outcomes.

Partnerships with Stakeholders

Tri-O is stakeholder-focused and outcome-oriented. It is based on earning and maintaining the respect and trust of stakeholders. Effective stewardship of fiscal and physical resources is part of earning this respect and trust. To do this we must actively demonstrate that outcomes are consistently achieved in measurable terms that stakeholders value and expect.

In the Minnesota Office of Admissions, the University's executive officers and the University's budget and human resource managers are among the Office's major on-campus stakeholders and partners. They are actively included in the Office of Admissions' strategic planning process. These partners have very demanding and sensitive jobs, are very talented and hard working individuals and want the same thing for the University that our office does.

Working with these individuals is especially important as the Office of Admissions considers major purchases or outsourcing of key software, equipment, or processes. In addition to the annual budget preparation process, we also periodically update stakeholders with the Office's goals, how our resources are being assigned and the opportunities and challenges that we face. We are very frank about successes and problems and work hard to demonstrate that the University is getting a good return on its investment.

The Office also works in partnership with University auditors. If we identify either an actual or a potentially significant problem we quickly disclose it. We call for outside expertise if it is not found in our staff. The University's audit staff has been a valuable resource and partner. In fact, one of the audit department's senior staff kindly served as a reader of several draft chapters of this book.

One of the top managers in the University's Department of Audits recently stated that the University's auditor is an independent score keeper. Their value as a unit is to serve as a catalyst for open communication and positive change. The Audit Manager pointed out that units in the University that have the greatest trust from the University's Executive Officers and Regents are those who make certain their work is transparent to the them. They share both the good and the bad with the University's major leadership. (Skovsted 2006)

It is probably human nature to resist having other people involved in our work and asking hard questions about what we do and the results we are achieving. However, in the Age of Outcomes this is the norm, not the exception.

We must understand that if someone can determine what our program costs the University, they can also probably determine the return on investment. The question for managers is whether they will lead this process or be led by others.

It is much better to be able to participate in placing our work and outcomes in the proper perspective and context rather than ceding this responsibility to those who may not fully understand our programs.

Tri-O is about playing offense, not defense. It is much better to lead the stewardship process. In order to do this, we must first make certain that we can *convince ourselves* that we are good stewards of the resources provided to us.

Remember, resources and influence will go to the programs whose managers demonstrate that they have consistently achieved the outcomes valued and expected by their stakeholders. Organizations and their leaders who either cannot, or will not, do this will wither away.

Demonstrating Good Stewardship

There are a number of ways to demonstrate good stewardship of the resources devoted to an organization. In this chapter, five options are considered:

◀ Getting out the good news
◀ Benchmarking
◀ Interacting with stakeholder advisory groups
◀ Working with strategic partners
◀ Re-engineering processes

Getting Out the Good News

Some people may consider making certain that stakeholders know about outcomes and positive developments as unseemly self-promotion. Self-promotion by itself is, in fact, unseemly and ultimately self-defeating. However, it is vital that managers keep stakeholders updated on the return on the organization's investments. People are naïve to think that this process is unnecessary. Good works and results are not enough by themselves. Stakeholders must know about them. If we do not proactively and regularly get out the good news, the best that will result is a neutral view of our work—but more than likely, our work will be looked upon negatively.

In order to have credibility in the *good news* process, it is important that stakeholders are informed about both the good and the bad. I keep my supervisors fully informed about the status of our office. I don't bother them with every issue and I don't make my problems their problems. However, I think it is important to give them a heads up on potential or real issues so they are not caught off guard. Being caught off guard makes people nervous and undermines their trust in you.

Periodic updates via e-mails and newsletters are good ways to get out the good news. Annual reports are another option. If you use these vehicles, I would caution you to not make the mistake so many of us make with these tools: Most of the annual reports that I receive are so worthless that I barely read them. Most are much too long. And most focus on process and activities, not on outcomes.

Do you think I am wrong about this? The next time you receive such a report, take a few minutes to read it in the perspective of process and activity versus outcomes. Most of these reports are simply a glossy and expensive waste of resources.

Effective updates must:

◖ Be short and simple.

◖ Look professionally prepared to garner credibility and confidence. This should not, however, be overdone or it will detract from the effectiveness of the report.

◖ Be relevant to the reader.

◖ Focus primarily on outcomes; not process and activities. Sell the steak not the sizzle!

Benchmarking

The importance of benchmarking seems to ebb and flow in higher education. I believe that it will become increasingly important because it is a specific, measurable way to demonstrate return on investment. Effective managers will get ahead of the curve and initiate benchmarking on their own.

Effective benchmarking takes a lot of work. It is important to place the items being benchmarked into context; it often takes a lot of work to develop "apples to apples" comparisons.

Having a peer group of institutions and offices greatly facilitates benchmarking. The Big Ten admissions directors have a very close relationship with each other. We frequently share information and periodically conduct benchmarking studies.

Occasionally, if we want to do an especially in-depth benchmark, I will work with several colleagues at similar peer institutions with which Minnesota does not have a competitive overlap. This makes sharing detailed and sensitive data somewhat easier.

Interacting with Stakeholder Advisory Groups

The Office of Admissions at Minnesota greatly benefits from the advice of multiple on-campus and off-campus stakeholder advisory groups. We meet with the advisory groups on a regular basis and ask them for their frank advice on a number of issues. The objective is not superficial public relations. The key is to get to know the advisory group members and develop a sense of shared purpose and trust so they will level with us about the good and the bad.

An additional benefit to working closely with stakeholder advisory groups is that people generally support what they help create. Having regular advisory group meetings to hash out sometimes very difficult and contentious issues is very helpful in building consensus and support.

Working with Strategic Partners

With the relative scarcity of resources in the Age of Outcomes, every organization must ask itself what core competencies it can build and maintain on its staff and those that it should outsource.

The outsourcing of functions has many pros and cons. However, I have found five keys to effective outsourcing:

- Don't build what you can buy. This is especially true with operating and application software.
- While functions can be outsourced, the control of key aspects of the function must be withheld. Remember an axiom of effective delegation—you can delegate authority but you cannot delegate responsibility.
- Genuine partnerships with strategic partners must be developed. Your success and theirs must be clearly intertwined and articulated.
- Outsourcing partners must be held to specific, measurable outcomes.

◀ If you work with an on-campus strategic partner, they must be able to demonstrate that they meet or exceed the performance of an off-campus vendor.

Re-Engineering Processes

Process re-engineering can be helpful in being effective stewards of our resources. Processes can get outdated and cumbersome and begin to resemble the barnacles on a ship. While each individual barnacle is small, together they can severely slow down and damage a ship. It is critical that an organization periodically review its processes to update and streamline them.

Process re-engineering is not easy and can be very tedious and time-consuming. It usually involves a detailed, step-by-step analysis of a process. There are various tools available to facilitate process re-engineering. Six Sigma (GE is a big champion of this) or Lean Manufacturing (championed by the Toyota Corporation) hold significant promise for delivering results. But because they are such time-consuming processes, I have not yet used them.

It is often helpful to bring in a person from outside the organization or unit to facilitate the process re-engineering. We have benefited greatly from the assistance of a staff member from the University's Service and Continuous Improvement staff who has significant experience with re-engineering.

Process re-engineering can also be politically challenging because it is imperative that sacred cows and strongly held opinions be addressed head-on. Process re-engineering often involves changing paradigms and cultures, which requires political skill and enormous tenacity and courage. However, it is absolutely vital that this process be periodically taken on or else the organization becomes calcified: a prescription for failure in the Age of Outcomes.

Beware the Bleeding Edge

The appropriate application of technology is essential to the efficiency and effectiveness in an organization. However, technology is often expensive, and can be ineffective if it is used incorrectly.

158

My view is that we should not become enamored with new technology simply because it is available. Organizations can become victims of adopting unneeded new technology. Managers must insist on the development of a business plan that can demonstrate the likely return on investment of employing new technology.

Effective organizations keep their processes as simple as possible and execute very well. New technology by itself will not give an organization a significant competitive advantage unless it is combined with effective processes and operational excellence.

The Dream House Diagnostic and Planning Tool outlined in Chapter 7 can be very useful to assess where new technology will fit in an organization's operations, and to determine if the technology will serve a core function, or is merely chasing a fad. (*See* page 128.)

That said, effective organizations should constantly scan the environment for new technology that it can effectively employ. The key to staying up-to-date and effective is to test out promising new technology on a relatively small scale to determine its return on investment. Test promising new technology, but don't bet the ranch on it until it has demonstrated that it can deliver on the expected outcomes. In the Minnesota Office of Admissions we are generally not the first adopters of new technology. Instead, we generally prefer to learn from the experience of a respected peer institution and then adopt the new technology that is still relatively cutting-edge but has some proven success.

The Importance of an Outstanding Budget/Human Resource Manager

A capable and effective outstanding budget/human resource manager is a must for any organization. I understand that, in some organizations, such functions are handled by more than one person. I have combined the roles in this chapter because that is currently the approach in our office.

The size and resources of each program determine if a budget/HR manager can be kept on staff. Regardless of whether the budget/HR manager is on your staff or elsewhere, you must work closely in partnership with this key person. The budget/HR manager should be a central member of your senior management team and be directly involved in all major program decisions.

The effectiveness of this key individual will help determine if your organization will play offense or defense in the critical areas of fiscal and physical resources. An effective budget manager must routinely provide managers with easily understood budget reports. The reports must enable managers to know the status of their budgets at all times. This empowers managers to act proactively without the fear of overspending their budgets.

Budget Allocation and Monitoring Processes

The Tri-O Budget Stewardship Component is not dependent on a particular budgeting approach. It does, however, require that managers recognize that resources are finite and valuable. Therefore, before resources are allocated to a project or unit, specific outcomes, including major benchmarks, the expected return on investment, and a timeline for realizing the return must be developed.

There are many budget allocation and monitoring approaches available. For some of our projects that are at the campus enterprise level, we enlist the assistance of budget analysts outside our office for

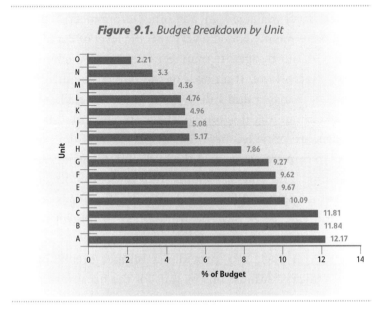

Figure 9.1. Budget Breakdown by Unit

160

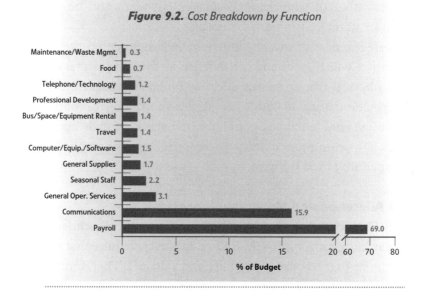

Figure 9.2. *Cost Breakdown by Function*

their specialized expertise to build very detailed and sophisticated budgets. In general, in keeping with the Tri-O basic assumption of keeping things simple, we build simple budgets using a programmatic approach rather than a detailed line-item approach.

We often allocate program budgets to associate and assistant directors. Tactical level managers in our office are expected to monitor their budgets frequently and at a very specific level of detail. As director, I work with our budget/HR manager to monitor the budget at the strategic or macro level. If an area of the budget is out of variance, the budget/HR manager and I drill down into the details of the budget to make certain that it is brought back into expected boundaries.

Two charts are provided here that display one of the macro tools that we use to gain an overview of the budget in the Minnesota Office of Admissions. The charts simplify our understanding of where money is being spent and helps us determine if changes are needed. The data and categories have been modified to protect the proprietary nature of this data.

Figure 9.1, on page 159, provides a budget breakdown of the Minnesota Office of Admissions by unit for the fiscal year.

Figure 9.2, on page 160, provides a cost breakdown of the functions of the Minnesota Office of Admissions for the fiscal year.

Summary

Excellent relationships with stakeholders are both crucial and helpful. That said, the consistent achievement of the measurable outcomes that they value and expect is ultimately what results in confident stakeholders.

Demonstrating good stewardship is not a luxury; it's a necessity. Remember—Resources follow the achievement of measurable outcomes!

10

PURPOSE

Defines how success
will be measured

OUTCOMES

Defines specific metrics
so that success can
be measured

Provides an early
warning system to alert
managers if a project is
off track, thus ensuring
timely corrective action

Tri-O

METRICS FOR SUCCESS

> *Not everything that
> can be counted counts, and not
> everything that counts can be counted.*

~ ALBERT EINSTEIN (1879–1955)

Imagine how frustrated spectators would be with an athletic contest that did not have a scoreboard and some measure, such as a time clock or innings, to determine the outcome of the contest.

Once the outcome plans for achieving an organization's goals have been developed, it is vital that specific metrics be put in place so that success can be measured. Without metrics, the result of planning is likely to be an activity or a process, not an outcome. Tri-O Metrics establish how success will be quantitatively measured and is a key component in establishing accountability. Metrics force us to define success and hold us accountable for achieving it.

Outcome Data is an Absolute in the Age of Outcomes

A January 19, 2004 *New York Times* article noted that:

The nonprofit sector is notoriously bereft of data, but in an era in which donors are increasingly demanding accountability and ways to measure effectiveness, organizations are moving fast to try to quantify themselves. (Strom 2004)

Ashburn (2006) commented on the status of institutional research in community colleges.

...[M]any experts in the field say community colleges continue to lag behind the institutional-research efforts of their four-year counterparts, although exact numbers are hard to come by...

What's more, until recently there was no financial incentive for two-year colleges to generate data on retention and graduation rates because state funds were based mostly on enrollment. But now many states dole out money on performance-based factors. And accreditors are demanding more information as they try to gauge student learning.

"We have emphasized more and more outcomes, not only student outcomes...but how the entire institution is doing," says Jean A. Morse, executive director of the Middle States Commission on Higher Education.... "What we've been working really hard to do is get our institutions to better define their goals and measure their progress."

A lack of measurable goals and accountability is not limited to individual institutions but is also evident at the state level. Hebel (2006) cited a report, " 'By the Numbers: State Goals for Increasing Postsecondary Attainment,' [that] was prepared by Jobs for the Future, a nonprofit advocacy group based in Boston."

Fewer than half the states have set specific, measurable goals for increasing their college participation, retention, or graduation rates, even as policy makers and institutions face pressures to improve higher education outcomes....

...[O]nly 23 states last year had set at least one numerical goal for increasing the number of students who enroll in college, who remain in college, or who complete a degree. Only 10 states had set numerical goals in all three of those areas.

Of the states that set goals, 15 had put in place some system for monitoring institutions' progress, such as through annual reports or report cards, the study found. Eleven states had offered clear rationales for the numerical goals they chose.

"States are spending $63-billion a year on higher education," said Marlene B. Seltzer, the group's president, "but if they don't quantify what they're trying to accomplish, it's going to be impossible to tell when they've succeeded."

Barriers to Setting Outcome Metrics

There are many reasons why managers do not establish effective outcome metrics for their organization or program. Let's review several possible reasons.

The "Pure of Heart" Model

I first learned of the "'pure of heart' model" during a talk by Dr. Eric J. Jolly, Director of the Science Museum of Minnesota, while he was participating in a panel on the pipeline for science, engineering, and mathematics talent. I subsequently read an article by Jolly, Campbell and Perlman (2004) which explained that the pure of heart model was developed by Tom Kibler and has as its main tenet "If my intentions are good and my heart is pure, then I must be doing the right thing…" (p. 18). The authors apply Kibler's theory to higher education, saying:

> *The "pure of heart model" often speaks to what motivates and inspires many of us in education reform. We have for decades wanted to do the right thing, to inspire, to teach and create pathways and opportunities for every child's success. Enough passion, in the right circumstance, can lead to success but too often it does not…. (p. 18)*

The "pure of heart" model is a very difficult thing to confront because I suspect that all of us can see at least some of ourselves in this model. The people described have honorable intentions and are very committed to their cause. We must, however, help them (and ourselves!) see that, in the Age of Outcomes, we must have a "pure heart" while demonstrating that we are achieving real and meaningful outcomes.

Case Study 20, "The Toughest Customers: How hardheaded business metrics can help the hard-core homeless" (on page 186), provides an example of how the "pure of heart" model can be translated into positive outcomes by the effective use of metrics.

Lack of Accountability and Incentives

A *Harvard Business Review* article entitled "The Ultimately Accountable Job, Leading Today's Sales Organization," notes that, "The best csos (Chief Sales Officer) will tell you that missing annual revenue and margin goals is simply not an option in their companies" (Colletti and Fiss 2006).

Can those of us who work in higher education say the same thing about our programs?

Some higher education programs seem to be more subject to accountability, or perhaps their outcomes seem to be more easily quantified. Football coaches are judged on their win/loss records; Development Officers on the dollars they raise; Admissions Directors on their incoming classes. Why is it that accountability for these programs is easily determined but many other programs are often deemed too complex to have just one person in charge and ultimately accountable for the outcome?

I believe a major reason is lack of institutional focus and/or will; if we saw real institutional will and focus applied to many other major university issues and programs that are currently applied to revenue sports, development offices, and undergraduate admissions, positive outcomes would increase dramatically.

Institutions *will* get focused and become accountable in the Age of Outcomes! The only question is whether we will lead the way in our programs or will others lead for us?

Lack of an Effective Mission Statement

I believe that many managers have trouble developing meaningful metrics for their organization because they have not developed a mission statement that has clear outcome expectations that can be operationalized. An effective mission statement is not a luxury but absolutely essential to getting an organization on the right track to consistently achieving outcomes in terms that its stakeholders value and expect. That's one of the reasons why the seven components of the Tri-O management game plan are inter-related and not designed as "stand alone" components.

Complacency

I believe that some higher education programs, especially those that are not in the daily spotlight of public scrutiny, are allowed to get by with relatively minimal expectations for measurable outcomes. Sometimes, higher level administrators seem to hold programs to the basic standard that they 1) stay within their budgets and 2) generate few complaints about the program that get bumped up to the institution's administration. Often in these circumstances, overworked and extremely busy top-level administrators will pick their battles and focus on the crisis of the day and overlook relatively poor or mediocre results. While this situation may continue to some degree, the Age of Outcomes will eventually drive accountability to all levels and programs in an institution.

Shifting Blame

Some managers duck personal accountability by diverting attention from their actions and responsibilities to the factors that they do not control directly. There is validity in this observation in many circumstances. Issues such as retention and graduation rates, cost of tuition, data security, campus crime are just a few examples of very complex issues where the contributing and determining factors are beyond the direct control of just one person.

However, one of the basic assumptions of Tri-O is there must be accountability, and if one person is not accountable, no one is really accountable. Until one person is designated to be accountable for each complex issue, measurable progress will be much slower than it has to be.

The Difficulty of Determining Cause and Effect

This is a corollary of "There are too many factors beyond my control!"

Anyone familiar with social science research understands that, unlike the physical sciences, it is often very difficult to demonstrate direct cause and effect. However, this must not stop managers from measuring results in as direct a fashion as possible.

One remedy is to take action and "Produce, Don't Perfect" and "Plan By Doing." The observations of Peters and Waterman in their now classic book, *In Search of Excellence,* seem very relevant. The authors found that many outstanding organizations employed mottos such as "Do it! Fix it! Try it!" or "Chaotic action is preferable to orderly inaction." Peters and Waterman (1982) suggest:

> *Getting on with it, especially in the face of complexity, does simply come down to trying something. Learning and progress accrue only when there is **something** to learn from, and the something, the stuff of learning and progress, is any completed action. The process of managing this can best be thought of in terms of the experiment and, on a more pervasive basis, the experimenting process.*

> *The most important and visible outcropping of the action bias in the excellent companies is their **willingness** to try things out, to experiment. There is absolutely no magic in the experiment. It is simply a tiny completed action, a manageable test that helps you learn something, just as in high-school chemistry. But our experience has been that most big institutions have forgotten how to test and learn. They seem to prefer analysis and debate to trying something out, and they are paralyzed by fear of failure, however small.*

In other words, do something! In the Age of Outcomes, the alternative is simply not acceptable.

Translating Stakeholder Expectations into Metrics for Success

Tri-O is stakeholder-focused and outcome-oriented. The entire Tri-O Management Operating System is designed to help organizations consistently produce the outstanding outcomes that their stakeholders value and expect. It is vital, therefore, that stakeholder expectations are translated into metrics for success so that goals, targets, and outcome plans can be developed to achieve these outcomes.

There are three steps to translate stakeholder expectations for the organization or program into Tri-O metrics for success:

◀ *Step One:* Develop metrics to determine how and when stakeholder expectations have been achieved. These metrics will be primarily at the strategic level.

◀ *Step Two:* List the key success factors that, when implemented, will track each of the outcomes expected by the organization's stakeholders.

◀ *Step Three:* List the outcome metrics that will define the actions to be implemented to achieve each of the expected outcomes. These metrics will be most often at the tactical or operational level.

Making Data Actionable

There are four keys to making certain that data can and will be used by managers.

◀ *Make it relevant.* The persons who will use the data must see how it is useful for their work or they will view the data as a collection of interesting (or useless) bunch of numbers. The effective manager takes time to demonstrate how the data will help a staff member with their daily work.

◀ *Place it in context.* A number without context has no meaning. Managers must help staff interpret what the data describes and its meaning for their work.

◀ *Make it prescriptive for action.* Tri-O Metrics are intended for use, not to be merely an intellectual exercise of collecting interesting data. Tri-O metrics help managers identify the next steps for keeping a project on track for success.

◀ *Focus on essential data.* A challenge in developing strategic and operational metrics is to limit the amount of data that is tracked to the metrics that are essential to the success of a program. The proverb that someone "cannot see the forest for the trees" is very applicable to developing metrics. The Pareto Principle— "the 80/20 rule" or the "vital few and the trivial many"—is a good guideline.

The metrics that you track must be useful or the very process of focusing on outcomes falls prey to the "process-oriented" trap. The Minnesota Office of Admissions is extremely data driven; however, we try to be very selective in what we track. That is why we term our basic success metrics "key success indicators." I must confess, however, that we periodically find ourselves asking if we need to track so much data and clean out the unnecessary clutter of data from "the garage."

Simons and Dávila describe a qualitative formula for "measuring" an organization's payback from its managers' time and attention. They call this formula Return on Management (ROM):

$$\text{ROM} = \frac{\text{Productive organizational energy released}}{\text{Management time and attention invested}}$$

Simons and Dávila (1998) have found that one of "The Allies of High ROM" is that:

> *[M]anagers know their key diagnostic measures—never more than seven at a time—by heart.... Why seven? If people are given too few challenges, there won't be enough variety in their work to stimulate creativity. If people are given too many challenges, they quickly suffer from overload. Seven falls between these two extremes.*

Case Study 17, "Professor Otis Redding Will Now Address The Class" (on page 183), and Case Study 18, "The One Number You Need To Grow" (on page 184), reinforces the importance of limiting the amount of data that you track.

Development and Production of Tri-O Data

As noted in Chapter 2, Tri-O works equally well in a program with a "staff" of one person or an organization with hundreds of people. Tri-O metrics can be developed in very simple ways. I state this with absolute conviction because I have, at times, used Tri-O metrics at very basic levels myself. I have developed graphs to guide my work using graph paper and colored pencils. Sophisticated graphing or charting software or highly trained data analysts and computer specialists aren't necessary to make Tri-O work for you.

Nonetheless, it is extremely helpful to have talented data analysts and computer specialists available to you for data that is relatively complex and data reports that must be produced on a recurring basis. Also, in the context of a Big Ten University, metrics that are adequate for day-to-day operational work may not be so when program outcomes move to the enterprise level where the level of sophistication and expectations about data are extremely high.

A major factor in using metrics to guide our work in Admissions at Minnesota is the talented staff that supports the collection, extraction, and analysis of the data. It is a team effort that involves operational and technical staff in the Office of Admissions as well as staff from the Provost and Institutional Research offices.

Levels of Tri-O Metrics

The three levels of Tri-O metrics are outlined in Table 10.1.

Table 10.1. *Levels of Tri-O Metrics*

METRIC	PURPOSE	OUTCOMES
Goals	Macro strategic level expectations	Defines how success will be measured
Targets	Operational level metrics	Guides the day-to-day work in the organization
Key Success Indicators (KSIs)	The individual data building blocks on which the Tri-O Metrics component is built.	Describes how success will be measured for an operational aspect of an organization

Goals

In Tri-O, goals are *macro* strategic level expectations.

In the context of the Minnesota Office of Admissions, goals are most often the enterprise-level macro numerical expectations set by the University's executive-level administration and our colleges for the incoming undergraduate class. The goals usually include metrics such as the size of the entering freshman and transfer classes and their expected academic preparation.

174

Targets

Targets are *operational* level metrics.

Once goals have been established, the macro metrics are translated into numerical *targets* that can be integrated into specific action projects that, when complete, meet the University's goals.

Key Success Indicators (KSIs)

Individual "key success indicators" (KSIs) are the *individual data building blocks* on which the Tri-O Metrics Component is built. A KSI is a metric that describes how success will be measured for an aspect of an organization's operation.

KSIs also serve, in a management-by-exception mode, as an early warning system to alert managers if a project is off track, thus facilitating timely corrective action. Conversely, KSIs also save time by indicating when a project is on track.

Figure 10.1 provides an example of a key success indicator used by the Office of Admissions at the University of Minnesota. This KSI tracks the number of ACT scores received from prospective students who have listed the campus as either their first or second choice with the ACT Corporation. This has become a critical item in assessing

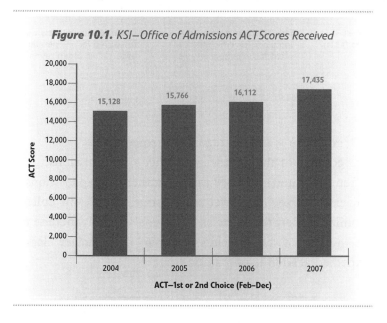

Figure 10.1. *KSI–Office of Admissions ACT Scores Received*

the current status of a recruitment year so this metric is monitored very carefully.

Many of our KSIs are drawn from data that is collected and summarized in a Filemaker Pro database. Other metrics are drawn from a data warehouse.

(Author's note: The data and categories in the following charts have been modified to protect the proprietary nature of this data.)

Key Success Indicators in Action

This section provides additional examples of KSIs that guide our work in the Admissions program at the University of Minnesota. The Office of Admissions conducts a variety of programs designed to encourage prospective students and their parents to visit campus. We have found that, for the most part, a prospective student will not enroll at Minnesota unless they visit the campus. Therefore, we proactively work to influence the outcomes in this area and track the results to make certain a particular program is successful.

The KSI included in Figure 10.2 tracks the number of individual prospective freshman students who attended a core visit program in the month of April. For example, if the projected number of visits

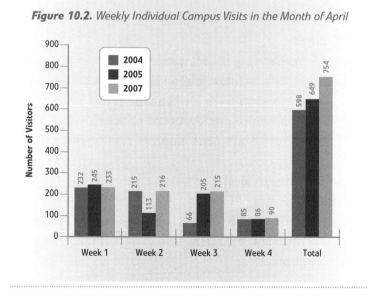

Figure 10.2. *Weekly Individual Campus Visits in the Month of April*

is running behind expectations, the KSI will alert us to this. Timely actions are then taken to increase the number of visits. Since campus visits are so important to the success of a recruitment year, we cannot afford to miss a target in this area.

Table 10.2 lists the four levels of display of Tri-O metrics, from macro to very specific.

Table 10.2. *Levels of Display of Tri-O Metrics*

METRIC DISPLAY OPTION	PURPOSE	OUTCOMES
Key Success Indicators (KSIs)	Individual data building blocks on which the Tri-O Metrics Component is built	Metrics that describe how success will be measured for an operational aspect of an organization.
Data Dashboards	A useful tool for organizing the metrics tracked by an organization.	Data dashboards aggregate data from a collection of KSIs to form a coherent view of a particular program, process, or activity.
"Trakbooks"	Collection of dashboards and various metrics that is combined into an Excel-based workbook.	Guides the operations of an organization.
Chart Room	Data displayed in a single room.	Enables managers to visually review much of the operational status of their organization or program very quickly.

Data Dashboards

A useful tool for organizing the metrics tracked by an organization is what the management literature often calls a "data dashboard." Data dashboards aggregate data from a collection of KSIs to form a coherent view of a particular program, process, or activity.

The Tri-O Metrics component employs two types of data dashboards:

◀ Strategic or macro level
◀ Tactical or operational level

Table 10.3 (on pages 178–179) is a *strategic* or *macro* level dashboard with an overview of our freshman recruitment process at a specific point in time.

Table 10.4 (on page 179) is a *tactical* or *operational* level dashboard that provides an overview of our freshman admissions application processing at a specific point in time.

Trakbooks

At Minnesota a collection of dashboards and various metrics are combined into an Excel-based workbook that we call a Trakbook. This term was coined by Dr. Ron Matross, Senior Analyst on the Provost's Staff, when he began developing our data workbooks.

For example, the Trakbook guides us in the enrollment management process as we shape the new freshman classes each year. Our enrollment management trakbook is a collection of highly detailed metrics that gives us a strategic overview of the freshman class in progress. The trakbook also enables us to drill down into any aspect of enrollment management that requires special attention.

The enrollment management team meets weekly during the processing season to review the trakbook and make strategic decisions to shape the incoming freshman classes.

Like most admissions programs, we are expected to bring in a class that is close to specified targets. For fall 2005, the freshman enrollment target was 5,305 new freshmen and we hit that target exactly. I must admit that enrollment management is both an art and a science and the excellent fall 2005 results involved a ton of good fortune. However, we simply could not manage a very complex holistic admission process with 26,000 freshman applications and 10,500 transfer applications without the data provided in the trakbook.

Chart Room

We have carved out space in the Minnesota Office of Admissions that has been designated as our "Chart Room." The data displayed in the Chart Room enables us to visually review much of the operational status of the office in about five to ten minutes.

We have placed a conference table in the Chart Room so that we can hold meetings and reinforce the importance of using the data there to guide our work. Our weekly enrollment management meetings, as well as various operational meetings, are held in the Chart Room.

Table 10.3. *Overview of Freshman Recruitment Process*

Class of 2007 Outcome Measures (Cumulative)	Total				Primary Market				
	F06	*F07*	*F07–F06*	*Dif (%)*	*F06*	*F07*	*F07–F06*	*Dif (%)*	
Inquirers	56,769	63,922	7,153	13 ▲	16,206	17,575	1,369	8 ▲	
Graded Inquirers	5,978	6,751	773	13 ▲	3,169	3,514	345	11 ▲	
Visitors	1,911	2,352	441	23 ▲	1,026	1,198	172	17 ▼	
ACT Score Senders	9,665	10,511	846	9 ▲	4,695	5,312	617	13 ▲	
Applicants	24,039	25,122	1,083	5 ◆	11,495	11,944	482	4 ▲	
Honors Applicants	2,004	2,576	572	28 ◆	1,100	1,383	283	26 –	
Confirmations	5,753	6,102	349	6 ▼	3,702	3,876	174	5 ▲	

Signifies change compared to previous week: ▲ UP; ▼ DOWN; ◆ NO CHANGE

Staff had the Chart Room walls painted with three coats of a magnetic paint and then painted with a finishing color that matches the rest of our walls. The magnetic background enables us to use small magnets to hang paper copies of our KSIs, data dashboards, and trackbooks on the Chart Room walls.

We designate certain of the KSIs and data dashboards as *strategic* level. Other KSIs and data dashboards are designated as *operational* level. We can walk around the room and first look at the strategic level metrics and determine if any item is out of variance in either a positive or negative manner. If an item is out of variance, we can then drill down into the operational level KSIs and data dashboards to glean more detailed information.

Tri-O Metrics Can Help an Organization Play Offense

A *Harvard Business Review* article on the role of an organization's chief sales officer (CSO) has relevance to all managers in higher education. Colletti and Fiss (2006), note that one of the sales chief's roles is to be a course corrector:

> *A sales chief always needs to be looking at some point on the horizon, then designing and redesigning the sales organization to help the*

Class of 2007 Outcome Measures (Cumulative)	Secondary				Tertiary			
	F06	F07	F07-F06	Dif (%)	F06	F07	F07-F06	Dif (%)
Inquirers	13,210	14,638	1,428	11 ▲	27,353	31,709	4,356	16 ▼
Graded Inquirers	1,508	1,837	329	22 ▲	1,301	1,400	99	8 ▲
Visitors	676	886	210	31 ◆	194	245	51	26 ▲
ACT Score Senders	3,854	3,814	-40	-1 ▼	1,116	1,385	269	24 ▲
Applicants	6,734	7,069	335	5 ▲	5,623	5,901	278	5 ▲
Honors Applicants	515	722	207	40 ◆	389	471	82	21 ◆
Confirmations	1,658	1,701	43	3 ▲	384	525	141	37 ▲

Table 10.4. *Processing Dashboard*

	Performance				Current Staff		Planned Staff	
	Backlog	Oldest	Goal Days	Current Days	Cont.	Temp.	Cont.	Temp.
X Week Goal for All Applications								
Scanning	0	–	1	–	1	0	1	2
Index	5	10/7	1	1	1	0	1	0
1st Stage Data Entry	151	10/5	6	3	2	2	2	2
Web Review	361	10/5	6	3	0	3	0	2
New Mail	408	10/5	6	3	0.5	1	0.5	1.5
New College Transcript	120	10/6	6	2	0.5	1	0.5	1.5
X Week Goal for Referring Complete Freshman Applications or Requesting Missing Information								
Waiting to be Processed	1,216	9/29	13	7	2.25	4	1	4
Missing Info Received	3	10/7	13	1	1.5	0	2.75	0
X Week Goal for Freshman Decisions								
1st Review	1,122	9/20	20	16	0	4	10	10
2nd Review	0	Up to date	20	0	1	0	6	0
Waiting for Letters	361	9/19	27	17	4	0	4	2

180

company get there. But the CSO can't take her hands off the levers or forget about the dials, or she might fail to respond to signs that a quick adjustment in sales priorities is needed. The best CSO's will tell you that missing annual revenue and margin goals is not an option in their companies. Consistent, predictable performance is expected, so they have to manage their organization for results, using short-cycle data and analysis....

The observation by John N. Pistone, a district manager running eight Home Depot stores on the east side of Atlanta, is a clear example of playing offense instead of defense. Pistone recognizes, as do all successful managers, that results at the end of the reporting period are the results of every hour, every day, every month of the reporting period. You can't wait to "make plans" at the end of the reporting period. You must play offense every hour of every day so that the results at the end of the reporting period do not put you on the defense.

"This is a quarterly business that we worry about hourly" (Grow, Brady, and Arndt 2006).

It is vital that benchmarks be set along the way to strive for specific interim progress and to make certain you are on track for success. Benchmarks are essential for playing offense.

The Tri-O system is designed to help organizations and its leaders better control their destinies. In this context, managers will sometimes choose to play offense and, at other times, defense. Chapter 11 describes how the Tri-O system can help organizations focus on making good things happen proactively instead of responding reactively.

Summary

Some managers maintain that their work cannot be quantified via metrics. But, as stated earlier, if someone can determine what your program costs the organization, they can also determine what results your program needs to produce. It's far better for managers to play offense by determining appropriate metrics for their organization or program than to play defense and have someone else do so for them.

Managing an organization or a program without effective metrics is like playing "pin the tail on the donkey." Pinning the tail on the donkey while blindfolded can be done, but a great deal of time, energy, and fiscal resources are wasted in the process.

In the Age of Outcomes, time, energy, and fiscal and physical resources are precious assets that stakeholders expect organizations to use effectively to produce measurable outcomes. The Tri-O metrics component is an essential management tool that defines how success will be measured and how to stay on track to achieve it.

Tri-O is not a grim, solely "bottom-line" focused game plan. Not everything is about the numbers, but Tri-O metrics are absolutely essential to the achievement of outcomes. Nonetheless, the Metrics Component, like the other six components of Tri-O, is not an outcome unto itself. Tri-O is ultimately about helping an organization manage for success.

Metrics, such as goals, benchmarks, and key success indicators, are essential for success. But the Tri-O system is not just about numbers, but about numbers that help staff to achieve outcomes. As important as metrics are to the success of an organization, its people are its most precious asset.

Resources on Metrics

The development of the current version of the Tri-O management system has been ongoing for over 30 years. Data has guided my work since the beginning of my career. I began to develop and implement specific metrics I call "key success indicators" for directing and evaluating my work in the early 1980s.

The use of metrics was inspired partially by *One-Page Management*, by Riaz Khadem and Robert Larken. Using metrics to proactively guide the management of an organization was also supported by reading about the work begun by former New York City Police Commissioner William J. Bratton and subsequently adopted and adapted by other police forces around the United States. The Compstat System developed by Commissioner Bratton is cited in several chapters of this book.

Kaplan and Norton's (1992) Balanced Scorecard concept is described by its developers:

*In the same way that you can't fly an airplane with just one instru-
ment gauge, you can't manage a company with just one kind of performance measure. Think of a balanced scorecard as the instrument
panel in the cockpit of an airplane.*

*It's a set of interrelated gauges that links seemingly disparate infor-
mation about a company's finances and operations. Together, they
give you a more complete view of how your company has been per-
forming, as well as where it's headed.*

*[The scorecard] allows managers to look at the business from four
important perspectives.... It provides answers to four basic questions:*

* *How do customers see us? (customer perspective)*
* *What must we excel at? (internal perspective)*
* *Can we continue to improve and create value? (innovation and
learning perspective)*
* *How do we look to shareholders? (financial perspective)*

I did not take advantage of the Balanced Scorecard concept until
around early 2003. Nonetheless, I recommend highly the concept. I
also recommend Kaplan and Norton's publications, including:

❨ "The Balanced Scorecard—Measures that Drive Performance,"
Robert S. Kaplan and David P. Norton, *Harvard Business
Review*, January–February 1992.
❨ "The Balanced Scorecard and Nonprofit Organizations,"
Robert S. Kaplan, *Balanced Scorecard Report*, Insight, Experience
and Ideas for Strategy-Focused Organizations. November–
December 2002.

A very insightful article that I also recommend is entitled "Coming
Up Short on Nonfinancial Performance Management," Christopher
D. Ittner and David F. Larcker, *Harvard Business Review*, November
2003.

CASE STUDY 17:
"PROFESSOR OTIS REDDING WILL
NOW ADDRESS THE CLASS"

LESSONS
FOR HIGHER   Having too many measures to track can be
EDUCATION   almost as worthless as not having any at all.
MANAGERS

These days, people know a lot. Thousands of business books are published around the world each year. U.S. organizations alone spend more than $60 billion a year on training—mostly on management training. Companies spend billions of dollars a year on consulting. Meanwhile, more than 80,000 MBAs graduate each year from U.S. business schools. These students presumably have been taught the skills that they need to improve the way that companies do business. (Webber 2000, p. 168)

In their book *The Knowing-Doing Gap, How Smart Companies Turn Knowledge Into Action,* Stanford University Professors Pfeffer and Sutton (2000) ask: "Why is it that, at the end of so many books and seminars, leaders report being enlightened and wiser, but not much happens in their organization?"

In an interview with *Fast Company* writer Alan Webber (2000, p. 168), Pfeffer sheds light on the above question by listing 16 rules that "...explain why, despite so much knowing, there's so little doing—and what you can do to get something done in your company." Rule 12, "Professor Otis Redding will now address the class," deals with the problems companies experience when they try to measure too many things:

There's an old saying in business: What gets measured is what gets done. What's happening today is the flip side of that. Measurement has become a tyranny that makes sure that nothing gets done.

I've developed what I like to call the Otis Redding Theory of Measurement, which is named for his song "(Sittin' on) The Dock of the Bay." In that song, Redding sings, "I can't do what 10 people tell me to do, so I guess I'll remain the same." That line sounds as if it could be about companies' misconceptions about measurement.

184

Companies have managed to convince themselves that, since what gets measured is what gets done, the more they measure, the more stuff will get done. Last summer, I met a woman who works for a large oil company, and she told me that the company has 105 measures for which she is responsible. So I asked her, "How many of those 105 measures do you pay attention to?" Her answer? "None." Because in the end, she's measuring so many things that she doesn't pay attention to any of them—105 equals zero.

Case
Study

....
CASE STUDY 18:
"THE ONE NUMBER YOU NEED TO GROW"

LESSONS
FOR HIGHER   Use data to improve your organization.
EDUCATION
MANAGERS   Simple is usually better.

Tri-O is stakeholder-focused and outcome-oriented. It focuses on both customers and outcomes, and expects loyal customers to market companies. A customer assessment system should use metrics that are streamlined instead of complex. In a December 2003 *Harvard Business Review* article, "The One Number You Need to Grow," Frederick F. Reichheld makes a compelling case that:

> *The path to sustainable, profitable growth begins with creating more promoters and fewer detractors and making your net-promoter number transparent throughout your organization. This is the one number you need to grow. It's that simple and that profound.*
>
> *Tracking net-promoters-the percentage of customers who are promoters of a brand or company minus the percentage who are detractors-offers organizations a powerful way to measure and manage customer loyalty. Firms with the highest net-promoter scores consistently garner the lion's share of industry growth....*

The following is from "The Idea in Brief" section of the *HBR OnPoint* article reprint:

Many companies—striving for unprecedented growth by cultivating intensely loyal customers—invest lots of time and money measuring customer satisfaction. But most of the yardsticks they use are complex, yield ambiguous results, and don't necessarily correlate to profits or growth.

The good news is: you don't need expensive surveys and complex models. You only have to ask your customers one question: "How likely is it that you would recommend our company to a friend or colleague?" The more "promoters" your company has, the bigger its growth.

*Why is willingness to promote your company such a strong indicator of loyalty and growth? Because when customers recommend you, they're putting **their** reputation on the line. And they'll take that risk only if they're intensely loyal.*

By asking this one question, you collect simple and timely data that correlate with growth. You also get responses you can easily interpret and communicate. Your message to your employees—"Get more promoters and fewer detractors"—becomes clear cut, actionable, and motivating, especially when tied to incentives.

CASE STUDY 19:
BRINGING ACCOUNTABILITY TO CITY HALL

Case
Study

LESSONS FOR HIGHER EDUCATION MANAGERS	Cities are complex, political organizations as are colleges and universities. Take a complex process and make it work for stakeholders via metrics.

Martin O'Malley was reelected as Mayor of Baltimore after his first term with 87 percent of the vote. As Thompson (2005) observes, this may be due in part to initiatives like O'Malley's CitiStat program—a kind of metrics system intended to encourage greater accountability from city agencies:

Thanks in part to O'Malley, Baltimore may be on the cusp of a renaissance. Its population slide—from nearly 1 million in 1950 to almost 650,000 today—has almost bottomed out. Commercial building permits jumped from $23 million in 2002 to $488 million last year (2004). Such news heartens Baltimore residents, who sometimes

186

jokingly call themselves Balti-morons for living in a city so grim it inspired NBC's Homicide: Life on the Street series. Drug use and crime in general are down, although O'Malley has only slightly dented the murder rate, which is five times New York's....

His urban innovations—primarily CitiStat, a computerized score sheet intended to make key city agencies like public works, housing, transportation, and police more accountable—have brought other curious mayors on pilgrimages to Baltimore. "We've moved from a traditional, spoils-based system of patronage politics to a results-based system of performance politics," O'Malley says.

Cities traditionally measure the performance of municipal agencies at annual budget drills. But CitiStat regularly confronts officials with citizens' complaints about broken streetlights or inadequate policing, allowing authorities to shift personnel and resources as needed. Every two weeks, managers head to see O'Malley or his top aides...to account for how well they have done just that. Workers who fare well can end up with Orioles tickets; managers who fall short have wound up with pink slips. The program has saved the city $100 million, O'Malley aides say. Last year Harvard University praised CitiStat for slashing overtime paid to city workers and cutting absenteeism in half at some agencies.

Case
Study

CASE STUDY 20:
"THE TOUGHEST CUSTOMERS:
HOW HARDHEADED BUSINESS METRICS CAN HELP
THE HARD-CORE HOMELESS"

LESSONS
FOR HIGHER   "Business" techniques can be used to "do good."
EDUCATION   Get the job done despite having many complex variables.
MANAGERS

These excerpts from an April 3, 2000 *Fortune* article by Cait Murphy illustrate how metrics and a business mindset can be used to tackle social issues, and net some surprisingly positive effects:

Roughly 200,000 Americans will sleep rough tonight; many have done so for years. The fact that this is happening in the richest country in history is a travesty....

...[T]here is a new way of thinking about homelessness whose language will sound familiar to Fortune readers. It uses terms like performance-based contracting, consumer-centric solutions, and ROI. Applying business logic to this intractable area of social policy is more than semantics. It is a revolution that both the public and private sectors are beginning to buy into.

Social scientists in the 1990s began to document the fact that the hard-core homeless are...a distinct market segment. On any given night, perhaps two million Americans are homeless, but only about 10% are chronically so (on the streets for a year or more). The chronically homeless are overwhelmingly male, and almost all have some impairment—mental illness, disease, disability, drug or alcohol abuse.

The second crucial datum is that life on the street is not cheap. That guy you've been passing in the box under the scaffolding costs the city of New York at least $40,000 a year in jail time, shelter costs, emergency room visits, and hospital stays. In Dallas, researchers put the figure at $50,000; in San Diego, as much as $150,000.

The new paradigm is that by focusing on the chronic homeless, cities can get people off the streets and spend no more and maybe less than they do by letting them stay there. "Cost-benefit analysis is a friend to the homeless," says Philip Mangano...who heads the federal government's Interagency Council on Homelessness. His goal is to end hard-core homelessness in ten years. So far, 200 mayors...have drawn up plans to do just that.

That's where business metrics come in. The first step is to establish a baseline of just how big the market is....

Next there are the consumers—the homeless themselves. The market research is done in the usual way: asking what they want. The typical response is emphatic. They don't want a 12-step program or a bed in a shelter. What they want is a room of their own.

Putting it all together has resulted in a strategic plan, Housing First.... The rationale is brilliantly simple: If you give people what they want (not what you think they should want), they might just accept it.

It seems to work. Pathways to Housing, a nonprofit, has placed some 400 chronically homeless, mentally ill New Yorkers in rentals and reports a success rate of 88% (defined as not returning to the streets for

five years), at a cost of about $22,000 a year per person. ValueOptions,
a managed-care provider, reports a 92% success rate with a similar
population in Phoenix, also using private housing....

188

....
CASE STUDY 21:
LOWER COSTS, HIGHER QUALITY

LESSONS
FOR HIGHER
EDUCATION
MANAGERS

Very complex, political, and once unsuccessful organizations can be transformed via effective leadership.

Metrics can make a significant, positive difference.

Quality can be enhanced with lower cost
through effective leadership.

Catherine Arnst's 2006 *Business Week* article, "The Best Medical Care
in the U.S., How Veterans Affairs Transformed Itself—and What it
Means for the Rest of Us," chronicles the dramatic turnaround of the
VA health system. This story has many important lessons for higher
education with the clear message that the government, and not just
private industry, can turn around a bad situation and make it a great
one. Also, an organization can focus on the patient and doing good
while implementing business-related approaches. Excerpts from the
article are as follows:

> *For decades, the VA was the health-care system of last resort. The*
> *movies Coming Home (1978), Born on the Fourth of July (1989) and*
> *Article 99 (1992) immortalized VA hospitals as festering sinkholes of*
> *substandard care. The filmmakers didn't exaggerate.... The huge sys-*
> *tem had deteriorated so badly by the early '90s that Congress consid-*
> *ered disbanding it.*
>
> *Instead, the VA was reinvented in every way possible. In the mid-*
> *1990s, Dr. Kenneth W. Kizer, then the VA's Health Undersecretary,*
> *installed the most extensive electronic medical-records system in the*
> *U.S. Kizer also decentralized decision-making, closed underused hos-*
> *pitals, reallocated resources, and most critically, instituted a culture*
> *of accountability and quality measurements. "Our whole motivation*
> *was to make the system work for the patient," says Kizer, now director*
> *of the National Quality Forum, a nonprofit dedicated to improving*

health care. *"We did a top-to-bottom makeover with that goal always in mind."*

The article points out that the VA does have some important advantages over the "...nation's fragmented private-sector system, where doctors work for hospitals as independent contractors, and third-party insurers pay the bills as they see fit..." At the same time, "The VA's mission brings with it some special burdens...Its patients are generally older, poorer, and sicker than those in civilian hospitals; there is also a higher prevalence of mental illness and addiction. And it has large numbers of patients with a malady that is much less common in civilian hospitals: post-traumatic stress disorder (PTSD)."

The results of the major makeover of the VA healthcare system are highly impressive:

> *The 154 hospitals and 875 clinics run by the Veterans Affairs Dept. have been ranked best-in-class by a number of independent groups on a broad range of measures, from chronic care to heart disease treatment to percentage of members who receive flu shots. It offers all the same services, and sometimes more, than private sector providers.*
>
> *According to a RAND Corp. study, the VA system provides two-thirds of the care recommended by such standards bodies as the Agency for Healthcare Research & Quality. Far from perfect, granted—but the nation's private-sector hospitals provide only 50%. And while studies show that 3% to 8% of the nation's prescriptions are filled erroneously, the VA's prescription accuracy rate is greater than 99.997%, a level most hospitals only dream about. That's largely because the VA has by far the most advanced computerized medical-records system in the U.S. And for the past six years the VA has outranked private-sector hospitals on patient satisfaction in an annual consumer survey conducted by the National Quality Research Center at the University of Michigan. This keeps happening despite the fact that the VA spends an average of $5,000 per patient, vs. the national average of $6,300.*

11

The Joy of
MANAGING FOR
OUTCOMES

People can be divided into three groups:
Those who make things happen.
Those who watch things happen.
Those who wonder, "What happened?

~ JOHN NEWBERRY/NICHOLAS BUTLER

The above quote is one of my all-time favorites because it's an ideal description of what Tri-O is all about—making things happen.

I identify with this quote because some days I see myself in all three categories. However, I am much more comfortable when I am making things happen rather than watching or wondering what happened.

Tri-O is not a passive system that encourages watching or wondering what is happening to an organization. Tri-O is about making good things happen and shaping the destiny of an organization.

Tri-O is a positive management game plan designed to help higher education managers experience the absolute joy of achieving consistent success by conquering the process and managing for outcomes.

CHAPTER 11 *The Joy of Managing for Outcomes*

Controlling Your Organization's Destiny

Sports enthusiasts can debate for hours as to whether a good offense or a good defense wins championships. In reality, it's probably having both an effective offense and defense that help teams consistently enjoy success. While sports teams with great defenses can often prevent the other team from scoring and thus prevent bad things from happening, great offenses make good things happen.

Allen Barra (2006) comments that television sports announcers often make generalized statements about football games that have no statistical basis. The following is Barra's myth number one: "Offense sells tickets, but defense wins championships."

> *As with most football clichés, there's no evidence for this one. The Indianapolis Colts led the league in points (430) and lost in the play-offs; but the Chicago Bears allowed the fewest (202) and they lost too. The previous season, the Colts also led in scoring but then got lost in the playoffs; so did the Pittsburgh Steelers, who gave up the fewest points. NFL champions have almost always been great on both sides of the ball. As football historian T.J. Troupe puts it, the adage should be "Great defense beats great offense—and vice versa."*

Unduly playing defense leads to inordinate fatigue and discouragement. While playing offense can be tiring, it's a much different type of fatigue. Playing offense leads to an organization better controlling its own destiny.

A *Minneapolis Star Tribune* article published near the end of college football's 2006 regular season featured the decline of the Iowa Hawkeyes football team which, at that point, held a record of 6 wins and 5 losses (Iowa ended the regular season at 6-6). At the beginning of the season, Iowa was considered to be a contender for the Big Ten football title. A 6-5 record led to criticism of the team's performance. The head coach, Kirk Ferentz, commented on what happens when even a recently very successful team has a losing season.

> *"The bottom line in sports is, if you're doing well and having success on the field everybody is warm and cozy,"* he said. *"If you're not, everybody is scrutinizing every little thing that could possibly happen!"* (Scoggins 2006)

My experience as a manager and consultant confirms that Kirk Ferentz's observation about sports is highly applicable to higher education administration. Colleges and universities have many brilliant people as major stakeholders. Consequently, these folks often have very strong opinions about why things went wrong and how to fix it. I have watched many managers who were the targets of criticism become discouraged, downcast, and often frightened about their job security. It is a gut-wrenching thing to observe.

A process and activity paradigm is about playing defense—watching or wondering what happened. Tri-O's outcome-oriented paradigm is about playing offense-making things happen by managing for outcomes.

One of the traits of a team that has to unduly play defense is that it is often described as being "back on its heels" because it is largely retreating instead of controlling its destiny. They are generally trying to prevent bad things from happening. Teams that are playing offense play off the balls of their feet because they are intent on moving forward to make good things happen.

In the context of higher education, it is important to be able to play both offense and defense. The seven components of the Tri-O Management Operating System include elements of both, with the basic premise being to play offense by managing for outcomes. Playing offense is much more joyful because it focuses on making good things happen and helping an organization shape its own destiny.

Playing Defense

The following adage, inscribed on a plaque aboard the M.V. Cunard Princess and slightly reworded for our purposes, offers wisdom useful in any professional context:

> *A superior sailor is best defined as one who uses his/her superior judgment to keep out of situations requiring the use of his/her superior skills.*

As the quote indicates, a truly superior sailor works to stay out of problem situations. Since playing defense focuses on preventing problems from happening, it plays an important role.

Avoiding the Avoidable

> *Considering the fragility of the human element, you make sure that no controllable physical element stands in the way of success. You leave all the possibilities for controllable physical mistakes to your competitor and organize for minimum defects in your own operation....*
(Michaelson 1987, p. 11)

Michaelson's advice is based on the reality that factors relating to people and their performance are often unpredictable. Therefore, one of the keys to developing a winning program is to control the variables that are more predictable and controllable. In a higher education context, this would include the processes followed and key ingredients such as consultation, budgets, and timetables.

The following are examples of why having a preventive process in place, and adhering to it, is effective management:

- Ethical and legal violations are deadly for an organization and its leaders.
- Overspending on a program's budget can cause serious consequences and lead to the branding of the program's leaders as poor managers.
- Constant customer complaints are corrosive and undermine stakeholders' confidence in an organization.
- Ignoring the input and expectations of an organization's stakeholders will lead to the downfall of a program and its leaders.

The Limitations of Playing Defense

Playing defense through process may help keep an organization out of trouble but it will not ultimately drive the organization to exceptional achievement and long-term success. It is essentially maintaining, not gaining.

Playing effective defense in the context of appropriate levels of consultation and adherence to meaningful processes is critical to the success of an organization. The Tri-O system is not about eliminating process but about conquering the widespread assumption by higher education managers that process is an outcome unto itself.

Playing Offense Gets Results

The importance of aggressively treating disease was reinforced by my internist, Dr. David Klevan, a physician on the staff of Health Partners in Minnesota. For me, Dr. Klevan is a modern day Marcus Welby—an excellent clinician and a very caring person.

Often, when I visit Dr. Klevan, I ask him what projects he is currently working on to improve the health and well-being of his patients and the community.

During one visit, Dr. Klevan mentioned that a top project was to help his patients prevent and better manage diabetes. Dr. Klevan referred to his approach as the "Klevan Full-Court Press." He shared with me the excellent results that his patients derived from managing their diabetes aggressively. It impressed me and reinforced the absolute importance of playing offense versus defense.

A *New York Times* article entitled "New Job Title For Druggists: Diabetes Coach" described a public health project in Asheville, North Carolina. The project enlists the aid of the town druggists to meet individually with their diabetic customers and coach them to more aggressively manage their disease. The following are excerpts from the article.

> *[The Times article notes that persons with diabetes]…face the formidable challenge of either managing their diabetes or suffering its potential ravages; blindness, organ failure, stroke.*
>
> *There are at least 21 million diabetics in the United States, and health officials have begun to despair of combating the disease because it involves getting people to do something much more difficult than taking their medicine or having surgery: altering their daily behavior, like their eating and exercise habits.*
>
> *For the past 10 years, the city of Asheville has given free diabetes medicines and supplies to municipal workers who have the disease if they agree to monthly counseling from specially trained pharmacists. The results, city officials say, have been dramatic: Within months of enrolling in the program, almost twice as many have their blood sugar levels under control. In addition, the city's health plan has saved more than $2,000 in medical costs per patient each year.*

"We get a four-to-one return on investment," said Barry Bunting, pharmacy director at Mission Hospitals, which runs the program in Asheville for about 450 city and hospital employees. "For every dollar spent on medicines or counseling about diet, exercise, and life style," he said, "the city saves $4 by preventing emergency room visits, dialysis, amputations, or other common complications of diabetes." (Urbina 2006)

Dr. Klevan's work and the *New York Times* article provide dramatic, concrete lessons that can be applied by higher education managers:

◀ You can "do good" while measuring outcomes.

◀ Changing the paradigm to playing offense instead of defense pays off.

Peter Drucker (1990) believed that:

[T]he most important task of an organization's leader is to anticipate crisis:

* *Perhaps not to avert it, but to anticipate it.*
* *To wait until the crisis hits is already abdication.*
* *One has to make the organization capable of anticipating the storm, weathering it, and in fact, being ahead of it.*
* *This is called innovation, constant renewal....*

Leader as Catalyst

I have been guided in my leadership development by a conversation I had years ago with Dr. Henry Shanfield, Professor of Chemistry at the University of Houston. Dr. Shanfield observed that the work of a good leader is similar to a chemical catalyst. The catalyst determines the direction and speed of the reaction. Similarly, the leader makes certain that the vision and direction of the organization is in place, and that the pace of the activities is sufficient to achieve the desired outcomes. Organizations, especially large ones, often succumb to inertia and playing defense versus offense. Thus, the role of the leader as catalyst is to speed up the pace of the action and ensure that the organization is on the offense and going in the right direction.

A leader must never let the organization or its human resources calcify. Therefore, the role of the leader as catalyst is to continually push the organization and its people out of their comfort zone so they may continually change and grow. This push must be done with respect and kindness.

The Joy of Managing for Outcomes

The ultimate security that any organization and its leaders have is the ability to consistently deliver outcomes in measurable terms that its stakeholders value and expect. This reality will require that a great many higher education managers change their paradigm from one of process and activity to that of outcomes. Tri-O is stakeholder-focused and outcome-oriented, with a focus on targeted action.

We can state with certainty: *Tri-O really works!*

Tri-O is a real-world, time-tested management operating system. Organizations that begin the journey of implementing Tri-O will *exponentially* increase their chances of not only surviving, but thriving in the Age of Outcomes. Tri-O enables organizations to experience the absolute joy of conquering process and managing for outcomes—making good things happen, and better controlling their destinies!

References

Abrams J. 2002. Write A Mission Statement that Your Company is Willing to Live. Harvard Management Communication Letter, cited by Tom Krattenmaker. March.

Abt, S. 2005. A familiar start to Tour de France: Armstrong in second. *International Herald Tribune.* July 4.

Ailes, R. 1990. Lighten up! Stuffed shirts have short careers; your best career move is to temper your ego and become easier to like. *Success.* 3(37).

Arnst, C. 2006. The best medical care in the U.S.: How Veterans Affairs transformed itself—and what it means for the rest of us. *Business Week.* July 17.

Arussy, L. 2005. The search for growth through innovation. *Customer Relationship Management.* July.

Ashburn, E. 2006. A mirror on 2-year colleges: Internal offices that collect data about the institutions have begun to show results. *The Chronicle of Higher Education.* 52(40).

Barra, A. 2006. Pro football's cherished myths, ten sweeping statements for which there is no statistical defense. *The Wall Street Journal.* August 26.

Beckwith, H. 1997. *Selling the Invisible: A Field Guide to Modern Marketing.* New York: Warner Books.

Bennis, W.G. and J. O'Toole. 2005. How business schools lost their way. *Harvard Business Review.* May 1.

Berry, L.L., A. Parasuraman, and V.A. Zeithaml. 1988. The service quality puzzle. *Business Horizons.* September-October.

Bruch, H. and S. Ghoshal. 2002. Beware the busy manager. *Harvard Business Review.* February 1.

Burrows, P. 2005. HP says goodbye to drama. *Business Week.* September 12: 83.

Butler, S. 1987. As quoted in *Pearls of Wisdom: A Harvest of Quotations from All Ages,* edited by J. Agal and W.D. Glanze, p. 36. New York: Harper-Row.

Byrne, J.A. 2005. The man who invented management: Why Peter Drucker's ideas still matter. *Business Week.* November 28: 96–106.

Byrnes, N. 2005. Smarter corporate giving. *Business Week.* November 28: 68–76.

Chanen, D. 2005. Sizing up a 2-month campaign vs. gangs; Minneapolis police point to fewer homicides and credit their Strategic Safety Partnership. But other crime numbers are still high. *Minneapolis Star Tribune.* November 27: 1B.

Cherniss, C. 2000. *Emotional Intelligence: What it is and Why it Matters.* Paper presented at the Annual Meeting of the Society for Industrial and Organizational Psychology, New Orleans, LA, April 15. Retrieved from: <www.eiconsortium. org/research/what_is_emotional_intelligence.pdf>.

Colletti, J.A. and M.S. Fiss. 2006. The ultimately accountable job: Leading today's sales organization. *Harvard Business Review.* July-August.

Collins, J. 2005. *Good to Great and the Social Sectors: A Monograph to Accompany Good to Great.* New York: HarperCollins.

Colvin, G. 2006a. What makes GE great? *Fortune.* March 6.

———. 2006b. Why dream teams fail. *Fortune.* June 12: 87–92.

Cosby, B. 2007. Quote downloaded from *QuoteDB*. Retrieved May 18 from: <www.quotedb.com/quotes/161>.

Covey, S. 2004. As cited by L. K. Johnson. Are you delegating so it sticks? *Harvard Management Update*. 9(7).

Davidow, W. H. and B. Uttal. 1989. *Total Customer Service: The Ultimate Weapon.* New York: HarperCollins.

DePree, M. 1992. *Leadership Jazz*. New York: Dell Publishing.

Dewan, S. K. 2004. New York's gospel of policing by data spreads across U.S. *The New York Times*. April 28.

Dillon, S. 2005. Universities fear control may be at stake. *The New York Times*. November 4.

Drucker, P. F. 1990. *Managing the Nonprofit Organization, Principles and Practices.* New York: HarperCollins.

———. 2006. Quote downloaded from *BrainyQuote*. Retrieved January 27 from: <www.brainyquote.com/quotes/quotes/p/peterdruck134881.html>.

ED. *See* U.S. Department of Education.

Edmunds, G. 2006. Leadership isn't a popularity contest. *USA Today*. July 11. Available at: <www.usatoday.com/money/smallbusiness/columnist/edmunds/2006-07-11-econ-small-business-usat_x.htm>.

Einstein, A. 2007. Quote downloaded from *The Quotations Page*. Retrieved June 18 from: <www.quotationspage.com/quote/26950.html>.

Enberg, D. 2005. Comment during a CBS golf telecast. April 1.

Farnham, A. 1993. State your values, hold the hot air. *Fortune*. April 19: 122.

Farrell, G. 2005. Dimon adds sparkle to JPMorgan Chase. *USA Today*. November 29. Available at: <www.usatoday.com/money/companies/management/2005-11-28-dimon_x.htm>.

Feder, B. J. 2005. Peter F. Drucker, a pioneer in social and management theory, is dead at 95. *The New York Times*. November 12: A13.

Fiedler, T. 2006. A retail remedy? Quick clinics are changing medicine and prompting debate. *Star Tribune*. July 16.

Field, K. 2006a. Colleges propose accountability system. *The Chronicle of Higher Education*. 52(46). Retrieved December 19 from: <http://chronicle.com/weekly/v52/i46/46a02103.htm>.

———. 2006b. Texas millionaire plots future of higher education. *The Chronicle of Higher Education*. 52(39). Available at: <http://chronicle.com/weekly/v52/i39/39a01601.htm>.

Finley, B. 2006. Sure he's a good coach, but can he recruit? *The New York Times*. November 8: D1.

Gawande, A. 2004. The Bell Curve: What happens when patients find out how good their doctors really are? *The New Yorker*. December 6.

Gendler, N. 2005. Buckley the engineer has his blueprint for 'heaven.' *Star Tribune*. December 9: D-1 and D-3.

Goffee, R. and G. Jones. 2001. Followership: It's personal, too. *Harvard Business Review*. Dec. 1.

Goleman, D. 2000. Leadership that gets results. *Harvard Business Review*. March 1. Available at: <http://dx.doi.org/10.1225/R00204>.

——— 2001. *What Makes a Leader?* Boston: Harvard Business School Press.

Goral, T. 2006. Higher education at the crossroads. *University Business*. July 1. Available at: <www.universitybusiness.com/ViewArticle.aspx?articleid=210>.

Grow, B., D. Brady, and M. Arndt. 2006. Renovating Home Depot: Skip the touchy-feely stuff. The big-box store is thriving under CEO Bob Nardelli's military-style rule. *Business Week*. March 6. Available at: <www.businessweek.com/magazine/content/06_10/b3974001.htm>.

Hage, D. 2006. Plotting a path toward best in public service. *Star Tribune*. January 22: AA1 and AA6.

Hamm, S. and I. Rowley. 2006a. Speed demons: How smart companies are creating new products—and whole new businesses—almost overnight. *Business Week*. March 27. Available at: <www.businessweek.com/magazine/content/06_13/b3977001.htm>.

————. 2006b. 37signals: Programming at warp speed. *Business Week*. March 27. Available at: <www.businessweek.com/magazine/content/06_13/b3977005.htm>.

Hebel, S. 2006. Report says states lack clear education goals. *The Chronicle of Higher Education*. 52(27). Available at: <http://chronicle.com/weekly/v52/i27/27a02404.htm>.

Herzlinger, R. 2006. Why innovation in health care is so hard. *Harvard Business Review*. May 1. Available at: <http://dx.doi.org/10.1225/R0605B>.

Heskett, J.L. 1998. Managing for results in the community of the future. In *The Community of the Future*, edited by F. Hesselbein, M. Goldsmith, R. Beckhard, and R.F. Schubert. San Francisco: Jossey-Bass.

————. 1999. *NYPD New*. Harvard Business School Case Study 9-396-293. Boston: Harvard Business School Publishing. Available at: <http://dx.doi.org/10.1225/396293>.

————. 2002. Developing a strategic service vision. In *Strategic Tools for Social Entrepreneurs, Enhancing the Performance of Your Enterprising Nonprofit*, edited by J.G. Dees, J. Emerson, and P. Economy. New York: John Wiley & Sons.

Hindo, B. 2006. Satisfaction not guaranteed: How cost-cutting can backfire when it ignites consumer rage. With tales of service shortfalls at Dell, Home Depot, and Northwest Airlines. *Business Week*. June 19. Available at: <www.businessweek.com/magazine/content/06_25/b3989041.htm>.

Humes, L.R. 2006. Broadcasting a new message about higher education in Nevada. *The Greentree Gazette*. March. Available at: <http://greentreegazette.com/President/load.aspx?art=68>.

Ittner, C.D. and D.F. Larcker. 2003. Coming up short on nonfinancial performance measurement. *Harvard Business Review*. November 1. Available at: <http://dx.doi.org/10.1225/R0311F>.

Jolly, E.J., P.B. Campbell, and L. Perlman. 2004. *Engagement, Capacity and Continuity: An Overview of A Trilogy for Student Success*. A report commissioned by the GE Foundation. Available at: <www.campbell-kibler.com/trilogy.pdf>.

Jones, D. 2005. 3M calls on Brunswick's former chief to be new CEO. *USA Today*. December 8: 3-B.

Kaplan, R.S. 2002. The balanced scorecard and nonprofit organizations. *Balanced Scoreboard Report*. November 15. Available at: <http://dx.doi.org/10.1225/B0211A>.

Kaplan, R.S. and D.P. Norton. 1992. The balanced scorecard—Measures that drive performance. *Harvard Business Review*. January-February. Available at: <http://dx.doi.org/10.1225/4096>.

Khadem, R. and R. Larken. 1986. *One-Page Management*. New York: William Morrow and Company.

Klevan, D. 2006. January 16 conversation with Dr. Klevan and project summary.

Kotler, P. and A.R. Andreasen. 1987. *Strategic Marketing for Nonprofit Organizations*. Englewood Cliffs, NJ: Prentice-Hall.

Kotter, J.P. 1990. What leaders really do. *Harvard Business Review*. March-April. Available at: <http://dx.doi.org/10.1225/R0111F>.

————. 1998. *What Leaders Really Do.* Boston: Harvard Business School Press.

Kouzes, J.M. and B.Z. Posner. 1999. *Encouraging the Heart: A Leader's Guide to Rewarding and Recognizing Others.* San Francisco: Jossey-Bass.

Lavelle, L. 2005. A rank offense to B-schools? *Business Week.* August 5. Available at: <www.businessweek.com/bschools/content/aug2005/bs2005085_1796.htm>.

Leber, L.H. 1987. As quoted in *Pearls of Wisdom, A Harvest of Quotations from All Ages,* edited by J. Agel and W.D. Glanze, page 7. New York: Harper-Row.

Lederman, D. 2006. 18 Yesses, 1 Major No. *Inside Higher Education.* August 11. Retrieved from: <http://insidehighered.com/news/2006/08/11/commission>.

Liswood, L.A. 1987. Once you've got 'em, never let 'em go: How much more costly is it to acquire a customer than to retain one? *Sales and Marketing Management.* November.

Lovett, C.M. 2006. Alternatives to the smorgasbord: Linking student affairs with learning. *The Chronicle of Higher Education.* 52(28). Available at: <http://chronicle.com/weekly/v52/i28/28b00901.htm>.

McCarthy, E.J. and W.D. Perreault. 1987. As quoted in *Strategic Marketing for Nonprofit Organizations,* edited by P. Kotler and A.R. Andresen. Englewood Cliffs, NJ: Prentice-Hall, p. 195.

McPherson, Peter and D. Shulenburger. 2006. *Elements of Accountability for Public Universities and Colleges.* National Association of State Universities and Land-Grant Colleges, Discussion Draft, July 6.

Michaelson, G.A. 1987. *Winning the Marketing War: A Field Manual for Business Leaders.* Lanham, MD: Abt Books.

Michelman, P. 2005. Preface to "How resilient is your company?" *Harvard Management Update.* 10(12). Available at: <www.orgdna.com/asae/downloads/HarvardManagementUpdate-December2005.pdf>.

Murphy, C. 2006. Targeting the toughest customers of all: Here's how hard-headed business practices can help the world's wealthiest nation deal with the hard-core homeless. *Fortune.* March 31. Available at: <http://money.cnn.com/magazines/fortune/fortune_archive/2006/04/03/8373067/index.htm>.

National Commission on Accountability in Higher Education. 2005. *Accountability for Better Results: A National Imperative for Higher Education.* Boulder, CO: State Higher Education Executive Officers. Available at: <www.sheeo.org/account/accountability.pdf>.

Nielson, G.L. and B.A. Pasternak. 2005. *Results: Keep What's Good, Fix What's Wrong, and Unlock Great Performance.* New York: Crown Business.

Ostroff, F. 2006. Change management in government. *Harvard Business Review.* May 1. Available at: <http://dx.doi.org/10.1225/R0605J>.

Padilla, H. 2006. Enforcement: St. Paul officer has no trouble meeting the quota on parking meter beat; Especially in downtown, parking violations far outnumber tickets doled out. *Star Tribune.* July 17.

Peters, T.J. and R.H. Waterman, Jr. 1982. *In Search of Excellence: Lessons From America's Best-Run Companies.* New York: Harper & Row.

Peterson, D. 2005. Lawyer builds profile in the cross hairs. *Minneapolis Star Tribune.* January 17.

Pfeffer, J. and R.I. Sutton. 2000. *The Knowing-Doing Gap: How Smart Companies Turn Knowledge Into Action.* Boston: Harvard Business School Press.

Phillips, B. 1991. KTRH (Houston, Texas) radio talk show (March 14).

Posner, B.G. and L.R. Rothstein. 1994. Reinventing the business of government: An interview with change catalyst David Osborne. *Harvard Business Review.* 72(3): 133–141.

Reichheld, F.F. 2003. The one number you need to grow. *Harvard Business Review*, December. The overview of this article was developed by the editors of the HBR as an OnPoint article, product 5534.

Rogers, W. Quote downloaded from *BrainyQuote*. Retrieved August 13, 2006 from: <www.brainyquote.com/quotes/quotes/w/willrogers164939.html>.

Salovey, P. and J. Mayer. 1990. Emotional intelligence. *Imagination, Cognition, and Personality*. 9: 185–211.

Schuh, J.H., M.L. Upcraft, and Associates. 2001. *Assessment Practice in Student Affairs: An Applications Manual*. San Francisco: Jossey-Bass.

Schurz, C. 1859. Quote downloaded from *The Columbia World of Quotations*. Retrieved February 6, 2007 from: <www.bartleby.com/66/79/48779.html>.

Scoggins, C. 2006. Running on empty. *Star Tribune*. November 16: C-10.

Sevier, R. 2005. Perfect plans? *STAMATS Newsletter*. xviv(1).

Simons, R. and A. Dávila. 1998. How high is your return on management? *Harvard Business Review*. January-February.

Skovsted, D. 2006. Conversation with Dennis Skovsted.

Strom, S. 2004. Many charities raised more money in '03, but costs grew even faster, survey finds. *The New York Times*. January 19.

Suters, E.T. 1976. *Succeed in Spite of Yourself*. New York City: Van Nostrand Reinhold.

Taylor, W.C. 2006. Your call should be important to us, but it's not. *The New York Times*. February 26.

Thompson, M. 2005. Wonk'n'roller (from The 5 best big-city mayors). *Time*. 165(17). Available at: <www.time.com/time/magazine/article/0,9171,1050335,00.html>.

U.S. Department of Education. 2006. *A Test of Leadership: Charting the Future of U.S. Higher Education* (pre-publication copy). Washington, D.C. p.16 and 20. Available at: <www.ed.gov/about/bdscomm/list/hiedfuture/reports/pre-pub-report.pdf>.

Urbina, I. 2006. New job title for druggists: Diabetes coach. *The New York Times*. December 30.

Webber, A.M. 2000. Why can't we get anything done? *Fast Company*. 35: 168. Retrieved July 12, 2006 from: <www.fastcompany.com/magazine/35/pfeffer.html>.

Weber, J. 2005. Waging war on hunger: How ex-marine Mike Mulqueen got a Chicago food bank in fighting trim. *Business Week*. May 16. Available at: <www.businessweek.com/magazine/content/05_20/b3933116_mz021.htm>.

Welch, J. and S. Welch. 2005. *Winning*. New York: HarperCollins.

Woollcy, S., J. Hcmpcl, and B. Lcak. 2005, Thc top givcrs. *Business Week*. November 28: 59.